GHOSTS OF HAMPSHIRE AND THE ISLE OF WIGHT

Peter Underwood

First published in 1982

Google Map

peterunderwood.org

EXECUTION

FREDERICK BAKER,

Who was sentenced by Mr. Justice MELLOR, at the Winter Assizes held at the Castle, Winchester, to be HANGED

For the Wilful Murder of

FANNY ADAMS, at Alton,

On the 27th day of August, 1867.

At the appointed time he was conducted to the scaffold & after a few minutes spent in prayer he was launched into eternity.

'Killed a young girl—it was fine and hot." These words will henceforth be as memorable in the chronicles of crime as the "I never liked him, and so I finished him off with a ripping chisel" of George Frederich Manning. "Killed a girl—it was fine and hot"—the cool confession and the commonplace remark appended to the admission form one of the most remarkable and one of the most appalling examples ever known of deep-dyed, ingrained insatiate, unrepenting wickedness. It is a self glorification in crime than a brutish ignorance that any crime had been committed and so calmly does the murderous clerk of Alton register his atrocity that one might be almost led to think that the murdering of children, and the tearing of them asunder, were quite as much a matter of form and business as making out bills of costs or engrossing deeds. To a wretch whose mind must be in a thoroughly non-natural condition, it may have seemed quite a natural thing to associate God's sunshine and the genial warmth of summer with the satisfaction of unutterable lusts and the indulgence of a taste for blood.

For
Chris, Maggie, Ben and Adam
with love

CONTENTS

Ghosts of Hampshire and the Isle of Wight	
Dedication	
Foreword	1
Preface	5
Abbotts Ann near Andover	7
Aldershot	10
Alton	14
Alverstoke	19
Andover	23
Arreton near Newport, Isle of Wight	25
Ashey Down near Brading, Isle of Wight	31
Basingstoke	35
Beaulieu	37
Bentley	48
Bishops Waltham	62
Bishopstoke	64
Brading, Isle of Wight	70

Bramshill near Reading	75
Bramshott near Liphook	93
Breamore near Fordingbridge	97
Buriton near Petersfield	99
Bursledon near Southampton	103
Chillerton, south of Newport, Isle of Wight	104
Chilworth near Southampton	109
Christchurch	113
Colden Common near Winchester	115
Crondall	121
Dodpits Cross near Newbridge, Isle of Wight	131
East Wellow near Romsey	133
Farnborough	134
Fleet	138
Four Marks	140
Freshwater, Isle of Wight	142
Froyle	144
Hartley Mauditt	146
Headley	148
Herriard, between Alton and Basingstoke	157
Hinton Ampner near Alresford	160
Holybourne near Alton	168
Kimpton near Andover	171
Knighton, Isle of Wight	173

Langrish near Petersfield	183
Langstone near Havant	186
Liphook	193
Liss	196
Lymington	199
Marchwood	201
Meonstoke	203
Nettlestone near Ryde, Isle of Wight	206
New Forest	214
Odiham	219
Portchester near Fareham	224
Portsmouth	226
Quarr Abbey near Ryde, Isle of Wight	233
Ringwood	235
Rowlands Castle	238
Rye Common near Crondall	240
Selborne	241
Shanklin, Isle of Wight	245
Sherfield on Loddon near Basingstoke	248
Southampton	252
Upham near Bishops Waltham	274
Southsea	277
Ventnor, Isle of Wight	278
Waterlooville	280

Wherwell near Andover	286
Winchester	288
Writers' Monthly Interview, January 1997	302
Wroxall near Ventnor, Isle of Wight	311
Acknowledgements	313
About The Author	315
Books By This Author	317

FOREWORD

I first came across Peter Underwood in Brecon by chance on my seventh birthday in the 70s. We were in the middle of a snow storm and the wind grew so strong at one point that the whole family bundled into the rickety old newsagent and toyshop next to the bridge for shelter.

There, on a rotating book stand were these fantastic books with such wild images and worrying titles that I was hypnotised: *A Host of Hauntings*, *Into the Occult*, *Ghosts of Wales* and *Ghosts of* many other areas. Fortunately for me, as I mentioned, it was my birthday and I don't think I've exercised that amount of emotional blackmail since. I left the shop with three of them and became completely uncommunicative for the whole of Christmas.

My mother disapproved entirely, complaining I was being morbid and probably wouldn't sleep. And she was right because night brought the silence needed for me to really concentrate on all these fascinating accounts of ghosts that moaned down in cellars and screamed climbing up old stairwells or appeared at the windows or empty houses. The line

"I'll just read one more and that's it," was given the nod of approval many times.

Oddly I recall being much more fascinated than frightened. Though occasionally a chapter would come along that made my blood run so cold, that I'd lie there too frightened to turn out the light, absolutely petrified while listening to every sound, convincing myself that I'd now drawn the attention of some local spirit that was now coming up the back lane or letting itself into the back garden to seek me out.

I once even dared to run across the room and peek down into the garden to check. Without knowing it back then, the muscle of imagination was being thoroughly exercised and seeds were being planted for the books I would write in the future. Many years later, after university, I was fortunate to become the editor of a magazine that interviewed authors and despite my rule of 'never meet your heroes' I suggested I interview the great man himself.

I still distinctly recall picking up the phone on the designated day and time, feeling excited but apprehensive that I was about to talk to a very important, if invisible, constant figure in my life; president of the Ghost Club, the 'Sherlock Holmes of psychical research', collector of ghostly legends, author and much respected member of the Society for Psychical Research but most importantly, the man who had fascinated and terrified me as a child.

I didn't know if he would be a nice man, a grumpy one or one that would be downright rude and self-important as some authors I have interviewed have turned out to be. Neither had I heard his voice so I didn't know if he'd be loud, booming and dramatic or eerily quiet

Then there was the click of the phone being answered and the most warm, friendly voice said my name and told me he was just reading and waiting for my call. I knew right then that it was going to be a great conversation.

I don't know how long we talked for but at many points we had to stop chatting and remind ourselves to get back on with the interview. We got through at least two hours worth of tape - much longer than my usual interviews. He spoke of times when people refused to go anywhere near pubs or hotels that claimed to be haunted, whereas now, business owners use ghosts to draw huge crowds.

He told me about a man who wired up his house to play spooky music, all controlled from switches built into his armchair, of nights in empty buildings recording footsteps and escaping cold spots that moved from room to room and about the time he saw his father shortly after he died.

His words brought back the snow storm and the rotating book rack in that shop so vividly. It reminded me of the absolute excitement I felt flicking through the pages of his books to see the new chapter titles and all the new horrifying or rousing illustrations. I read Peter Underwood, book after book, year after year and I hope that I am able to make my own readers feel that way about my own.

Alan Williams
June 2018, London

[Alan Williams is the author of The Blackheath Seance Parlour (2013), *a mixture of gothic horror and historical fiction, with an additional injection of humour. He conducted an interview with Underwood in 1997, which appeared in a publication he was editor of at the time -* Writers' Monthly *- and is reproduced as a coda to this book.]*

PREFACE

Hampshire is a rewarding and happy hunting ground for the pursuer of ghosts and legends and I cannot claim to have more than skimmed the surface for there is a great deal more material that I shall continue to collect — hopefully for another volume! What I have endeavoured to do is to present a representative selection of legends, poltergeist cases, hauntings and well-attested ghost stories from most parts of the county and in doing so I have produced many ghost stories that have never been published previously and some, such as those associated with Marwell Hall and Bramshill that have not previously been fully explored. If I have strayed a little outside the present boundaries of Hampshire I hope I may be forgiven.

Ghosts and haunted houses have interested me for almost as long as I can remember, probably because my maternal grandparents lived in a haunted house — but that is another story. For many years now I have collected, investigated and explored stories of ghosts and hauntings with, I hope, an open mind and always keeping my feet firmly on the ground. During the many hours, in daylight and in darkness, that I have spent in haunted rooms and haunted localities, I have heard and seen enough to convince me that some houses are haunted and some people do see ghosts. If you are one of these fortunate people or if you know of a haunted house, I shall be very interested to hear from you.

This exploration of haunted Hampshire has been a fascinating journey of discovery and I am deeply grateful to all the kind people who have welcomed me to their homes and patiently related their ghost stories and their legends. These stories are part of our heritage and deserve to be recorded and preserved: I have tried to do justice to every haunted house in Hampshire but I feel sure that some have escaped my net...

In a world of mechanisation, standardisation and automation it is a sobering thought that there are still some things that we cannot completely explain. And now let me take you by the hand and lead you through the haunted houses of Hampshire and the Isle of Wight.

Peter Underwood
The Savage Club
Berkeley Square
London W1

ABBOTTS ANN NEAR ANDOVER

There is a five-hundred-year-old inn here that was for centuries a cottage and the Cottage Bar is a pleasant reminder of the original building. Twenty years ago the place was derelict and Charles Bowyer bought the place, renovated it into a substantial home and then changed it into a delightful inn. And throughout the changes there was activity that was put down to a ghost.

There are persistent stories of a London society lady holding wild parties and conducting 'strange goings-on' in the eighteenth century... a tunnel is reputed to run from the cellar to a nearby river and although this was probably a conduit of some kind, it could well have been utilised for some quite different and unspecified purpose.

A hundred years or more later there was a lot of talk about a ghostly black dog that haunted the area and it is said that one farm worker, encountering the unfamiliar animal a second time within a few days, took a swing at it with his stick — which went through the 'animal' and had more effect on the man wielding the stick than on the ghost animal!

More recently footsteps have been heard inside the building, seemingly walking up and down stairs. Doors have closed by themselves, sometimes violently although there has been no draught or wind that might have caused them to do so.

Once or twice a vague form, possibly female, has been seen in the vicinity of the stairs and once a barman said he distinctly saw such a figure when all the occupants of the place were accounted for and no strangers were on the premises.

For years after the practice was abandoned elsewhere an old funeral custom was still carried out at Abbotts Ann. When a young girl died, 'the white flower of a blameless life', her companions would accompany her to the grave carrying a chaplet or 'virginal crown' and a pair of large white paper gloves, borne on a wand over the coffin. After burial these 'virginal crowns' were preserved in the little church with its handsome gallery and along the cornice of the ceiling they would hang from little shields bearing names and dates, some thirty or forty of them, not that many years ago. Gilbert White mentions the custom having existed at Selborne and at Farringdon and Shakespeare refers to the practice at the burial of Ophelia in *Hamlet*; he calls them virgin crants.

Another Hampshire church, not far away, has long had a custom concerning weddings. On arrival the wedding party would be carefully shepherded in through the north door and, after the ceremony, out by the door on the south side. Should this tradition be disregarded, it was said, some dreadful disaster would befall the bride within a year.

ALDERSHOT

Here there are ghosts of yesterday and ghosts of today. One of the oldest buildings in Aldershot is haunted, so is a modern hospital, and a lane that was once in the middle of the country.

The site of the ancient Fox and Hounds Inn is now occupied by a charming and weathered house and it is said that strange happenings have taken place, there for centuries, most of them believed to be attributable to a ghost known as Old Mother Squalls.

There certainly was an old woman, who was generally regarded as a witch, living in a hut nearby in 1840 and her pranks and activities left no doubt in the minds of those who crossed her that she had supernormal powers. According to contemporary accounts she could plait the mane or tail of a horse in an instant, curl or twist a cow's tail just as quickly, and terrify a dog or a cat to such an extent that these animals would race away with their tails between their legs.

In the 1850s determined efforts were made to outwit the witch, or ghost, but she always came off the winner, distracting all and sundry with strange noises, sudden appearances and weird happenings.

The big day in Mother Squalls life came in February 1675 when she was hastily summoned to the inn at dead of night to attend a confinement. It was a secret birth that could have changed the course of history and been the cause of anyone who was concerned with the affair, losing their heads... the woman who gave birth was Nell Gwynne, the father of the child was Charles II, but the illegitimate boy was born dead.

In the dark silence of the early morning a little box was buried under the yew tree just inside the church gate; the village priest having been aroused from his bed to perform the required ceremony. There has always been a persistent rumour that the Parish Church of Aldershot received a grant from Charles II for the manner in which this little episode in history was conducted and that the grant would continue as long as the yew tree flourished; but alas, the church records reveal no such transaction.

Yet there are those who remember stories of dark figures seen in the vicinity of the old yew on February nights, figures that melt and disappear inexplicably; and the residents in the old house report strange noises from time to time: a tapping sound such as might be made by an old woman with a stick; bell-ringing which is never explained and the occasional dragging footsteps of an elderly person — such noises were last recorded in 1971 and 1976.

A few years ago, following a car accident, my wife was mistaken for a ghost at the Cambridge

Military Hospital where there has long been talk of a ghost on the women's ward, a ghost they call the Grey Lady.

During the course of a short history of the hospital written in 1974, it is stated that the legend of the Grey Lady seems to stem from a Sister in the Queen Alexandra Imperial Nursing Service who inadvertently administered a fatal dose to a patient and in her remorse afterwards committed suicide by throwing herself over the hospital balcony.

The Grey Lady herself is said to have been seen and heard by patients and staff at the century-old hospital many times, apparently making her rounds as she did so often during her lifetime. Her last recorded appearance was in 1969 when she was seen by a night orderly sergeant. Often, the Hospital Administrative Office told me in 1980, the ghost seems to appear when the staff are under pressure of some kind, extremely busy perhaps, or understaffed; a ghost that attempts to be benign and comforting but can be very frightening for those who encounter it.

Ward 13 used to have a balcony but the original hospital has been built round and various floors and corridors added but it is still most frequently in the vicinity of the ominously numbered Ward 13 that the ghostly Grey Lady walks.

Beacon Hill, to the west of Aldershot, was one of many such places that were used to pass on warn-ings to London and other places at time's of great victory, terrible disaster or possible danger. So in 1815 a bonfire blazed with news of Wellington's success at Waterloo and an army runner carried the news to Aldershot.

It was wild country thereabouts in those days and as the messenger pounded down the rough track, the thud of his heavy boots suddenly ceased as he was set upon and murdered by wayside thieves. Today the track has become Alma Lane but still on quiet winter nights the ghost runner is occasionally heard thudding down the deserted lane and then suddenly, as happened more than a century-and-a-half ago, the sounds abruptly cease and the night resumes its silence.

ALTON

A country town where once lived Edmund Spenser, that prince of poets who knew Walter Raleigh and was presented by him to Queen Elizabeth I; the man who wrote the immortal 'Faerie Queene' which he dedicated to the Queen; the poet's poet whose sudden death in 1599 gave rise to a crop of legends. His house, in Amery Street, is now two cottages and bears a tablet saying that Spenser lived there in 1590, before he was married. From time to time there are reports of the lonely shade of a little man with short hair and dressed in Elizabethan garb having been seen in the vicinity of the house where he may well have 'enjoyed his muse, in this delicate sweet air, and writ a good part of his verse', as John Aubrey has put it.

The Parish Church of St Lawrence is very old and full of interest and beauty with its crude carvings of dragon, dove, ass, hyena and cockerel by men who may have fought at the Battle of Hastings. Six hundred years later Royalist Colonel Boles made his last stand here against Sir William Waller and his Cromwellian troopers and the bullet holes and marks on the pillars, doorways and the church door itself bring the Civil War dramatically to life. Visitors to the church have become so immersed in the atmosphere of this stirring historical episode that they have actually felt that the church was filled with struggling and fighting men and they have seemed to hear the sounds of battle such as must have filled this building more than three hundred years ago.

Edmund Spenser's house

Ten years ago, in May 1970, my old friend Dorothea St Hill Bourne, historian and student of psychic phenomena, met one parishioner who said he had spoken to at least half-a-dozen people who had experienced this phenomenon and she herself had the overwhelming impression that the church was full of grim fighting men, one evening during a church service.

A more tranquil influence from some forgotten episode from the past is reflected by the very strong smell of lilies-of-the-valley that has been reported occasionally in the main porch of Alton Church, often completely out of season. In August 1971 it was experienced by a party of five people visiting the church at 11.00 in the morning. Dr W.S. Scott, the great authority on Joan of Arc, was in the party and he told me that he searched diligently for any material cause for the overpowering scent. But he was completely baffled. At the time no one in the party was aware that on occasions this sweet scent had been reported by other visitors.

Alton Parish Church

The gentle ghost of Fanny Adams has also been seen at Alton. One August day in 1867 Fanny Adams, a nine-year-old girl, was brutally murdered by Frederick Baker, a local solicitor's clerk. He left her savagely dismembered body in a field near her home, writing casually in his diary afterwards, *'August 24, Saturday. Killed a young girl. It was fine and hot.'* Frederick Baker was arrested, found guilty and hanged at Winchester; his callous attitude to his crime reflected by the broadsheet announcing his execution, now in the Curtis Museum at Alton. The ghost of his victim has been seen in the area where the murder took place but the name of Fanny Adams lives on in a different connection.

At the time that the murder was making headline news the Royal Navy was, for the first time, being issued with tinned meat instead of the traditional salt ship's biscuit. The sailors did not take kindly to the change and they quickly associated the two unconnected occurrences. With wry naval humour they suspected that the contents of the tins were related to the dismembered body of Fanny Adams and since the poor girl's initials represented a common profanity meaning 'sweet nothing', the phrase 'Sweet Fanny Adams' was adopted by the men and soon passed into common usage where it remains to this day.

The sound of an invisible dog barking and scratching and whining is reported to haunt a 15th-century former coaching inn in the centre of the town. The haunting at the Crown Inn is supposed to date from the time that a previous owner cruelly destroyed his dog by smashing its head against a brick fireplace in the dining-room and then throwing the body on the fire. This fireplace was afterwards bricked-up but during alterations in 1967 workmen broke down a false wall near the original dining-room hearth and there they discovered the skeleton of a dog. After these remains were buried the ghostly barking was heard less frequently but there appear to be other ghosts at the inn, including a maidservant from long ago, but who she is and why she haunts the inn nobody seems to know.

The Crown Inn

ALVERSTOKE

An officer in the Royal Navy has related this experience which happened to him when he was a boy, an incident in his life which he has never forgotten.

"The house was an old one, on a common, with a walled garden and a small lawn. The windows had small, square, old-fashioned panes and on one of them a former occupant or visitor had scratched her name, 'Mary Carmoys'. The house had been much altered and enlarged over the years and had probably been once no more than a cottage. The former stable was not used in the days that we were there, except as a coal cellar, and the people who were there before us did not keep horses either."

The officer's family rented the house furnished and they had been there for several years before anything unusual took place. The father was away at sea and there remained in the house the mother, the children and the resident servants. The officer continues his story:

"One evening I had not been feeling well and my mother suggested that I had better go to bed. I went upstairs with her and she left me at the top of the landing stairs while she went up three steps to the right and along a passage to the entrance of the bathroom, where a table always stood at night, on which the bedroom candles were kept.

'You wait here,' she said; 'I'll go and get a light.'

The hall lamp was not yet lighted, nor the landing lamp, so it was dim, being close on October, about six in the evening.

As I say, my mother left me while she went to light a candle. When she had gone and I was waiting for her to come back, I saw facing me a man dressed as a sailor in a blue jersey and stocking cap, who stared at me very intently. His expression frightened me, and his face was peculiarly repulsive. He looked like a particularly villainous specimen of the loafers one sees on the Hard at Portsmouth.

As I watched him, almost shaking with fright, I heard my mother returning. As she came down the steps the man vanished quite suddenly. She noticed immediately that I was upset and asked what was the matter. I said, 'There's a man standing in the passage.'

'Oh, nonsense!' said my mother; but nevertheless she hunted the whole house and found no one.

I was so thoroughly frightened at seeing the man that nothing would induce me to sleep in my own room, and so I slept with my mother that night. I may add that she was very religious and extremely sceptical of anything in the nature of ghosts, but my terror was so evident that she saw I was not humbugging or telling a lie. She had at first believed that I had seen a real man — perhaps a tramp who had broken into the house — but after she had made a thorough search and found nothing, she did not know what to make of the matter.

Six years later, when we had moved to Devonshire, the conversation turned on servants, and I asked my mother why my former nurse and the cook had left the house at Alverstoke so suddenly. She told me that they had both said they had seen the man I had seen, each on different occasions, but all within a few days of my seeing him, and they had left the house at once. My mother added that she had since heard that the house was reputed to be haunted by a sailor who was supposed to have been murdered in the house over some dispute concerning a girl.

The house, which stood close to the creek, had been a well-known resort for smugglers and this was borne out by subsequent events. The next tenant after ourselves kept horses, and the stable was accordingly cleaned out and used for its original purpose. One day, one of his horses fell into a pit on the way to the stable, the ground having given way, and there was found a regular smugglers' hiding-place of the old type, such as you read about in stories.

That ends my story, but I can assure you I shall never forget seeing the ghost as long as I live. I can remember his horrible malignant expression to this very day."

ANDOVER

Phantom horses are commonplace but there are fewer reports of ghostly pigs, yet there is one very early and very curious story from Hampshire. On Christmas Eve 1127 (or was it 1171? the year is uncertain), it is said that 'a certain priest, at midnight, in the presence of the whole congregation, was cast down by lightning, with no other injuries. . . but what looked like a pig was seen to run to and fro between his feet.' The officiating priest struck dead at midnight and a ghostly pig careering about the church! Alas, the Norman church where this arresting incident reportedly took place is no more, having been pulled down due to its 'ruinously unsafe condition'; a report belied by the difficulties with which the so-called ruin was eventually demolished. One archway remains to remind us of an incident unique among the ghosts of Hampshire.

The White Hart Hotel in Bridge Street is an old building with stories of Charles I having stayed there and, some years ago, there were stories of ghostly happenings.

A figure described as 'a tall lady in a dress of dark green' was reportedly seen by a number of disinterested visitors who were unaware that such a phantom form was associated with the hotel.

And always the witnesses said they saw the figure 'gliding' along an upstairs corridor. Vague shapes and forms were also reported on the ground floor, in several rooms. One account described a 'nearly white, semi-transparent figure without any definite outline' that drifted through a doorway. And the inevitable unexplained footsteps were heard, usually in the evening and sometimes visitors were so upset by the noises that they secured their doors after ascertaining that no living person was in fact outside their rooms.

Author Tony Raper tells that there is an old manor house near Andover that is haunted by the ghost of a Cavalier. It seems that during the Civil War a Cavalier was a guest at the manor when a party of Roundheads swept up to the house. Hastily the Cavalier hid in the chimney but the Roundheads were up to that kind of thing and while some made their presence known by diligently searching everywhere inside the house, others crept quietly onto the roof and when the Cavalier's hands appeared out of the chimney he had painfully climbed, they cut off his fingers and the Cavalier dropped to his death on the hearth below where a bloodstain that could not be removed was shown for many years as proof of the story. The ghostly Cavalier has been seen in the vicinity of the room where, for the last time in his earthly life, he hid in the chimney.

ARRETON NEAR NEWPORT, ISLE OF WIGHT

It is no exaggeration to describe Arreton Manor as one of the most beautiful and historic houses on the Isle of Wight. Beautiful it certainly is, strangely beautiful it has been called, with an atmosphere of peaceful happiness; and it has at least twelve hundred years of history.

There was a manor house here before Edward the Confessor acquired the place in 1050. Barons have lived here, and knights, the Church has owned it. Now it slumbers, occasionally producing a quite inexplicable scent of incense; more rarely a chanting of monks; more rarely still the apparition of a woman in a tight-waisted dark red dress and even more rarely still the phantom of a child who witnessed a murder.

Back in Elizabethan times the manor was owned by the wealthy Leigh family and when old Barnaby Leigh lay ill in bed, but not yet dying or anywhere near it, his son John, over-anxious to inherit the wealth and property of his father, smothered the old man with a pillow. But the deed was inadvertently witnessed by John's young sister Annabelle and her brother, in a panic, dragged her upstairs and pushed her through a high window to her death. It is said that there is an area of coldness in that room that nothing can remove.

The ghost of little Annabelle has been seen and heard at Arreton Manor. From time to time a little figure in a blue dress with white slippers, criss-cross laced with ribbon, has been glimpsed briefly walking quietly through various parts of the house and in the garden on fine evenings. Sometimes a little cry like 'Mamma, Mamma. . .' accompanies the apparition but mainly it is a quiet, peaceful ghost returning to the lovely house she once knew.

Arreton Manor

My friend Margaret Royal, who is a mine of information on the ghosts of Bath, told me in July 1976 about a visit to Arreton Manor by Mr Elvin, an archivist at Lincoln, Mrs Elvin and Mr Arthur Start in May that year. 'In an upstairs bedroom Mrs Elvin felt a feeling of unease. Mr Stark experienced a more intense feeling and he also felt a pressure on his shoulder. Mr Elvin was unaffected. A few weeks previously a small girl on the stairs saw a little girl in a long blue dress vanish into a wall. A monk has also been seen and mediaeval music has been heard by a number of visitors...'

This beautiful house is open periodically to visitors and on occasions strangers ask about the sweet little girl in a blue dress that they have seen, a child who seemed to vanish inexplicably. Once a child came running to her mother saying she had seen a little girl in a blue dress and when she had walked towards her, she had disappeared into a brick wall...

Mrs Ivy Welstead, receptionist at Arreton, has both seen and heard the ghost of Annabelle. One evening, when she was thinking of nothing in particular, she heard footsteps and then a cry like 'Mamma, Mamma...' She ascertained that all the children then in the house were in bed and asleep.

Then, another evening, in the autumn, she thought she heard a sound and looking up saw the figure of Annabelle standing on the top step of the main staircase. The electric light was on and Mrs Welstead has no doubt about what she saw. The figure appeared to be exactly as it had been described by other people who claimed to have seen it: a little girl in a blue dress that reached almost to the white shoes; a sweet little innocent face with fair hair falling to the shoulders in tight curls. The figure remained quite still while Mrs Welstead took it all in and then it slowly faded away. In the garden too Mrs Welstead says she has caught a brief glimpse of the same form and heard that childish voice that echoes long in the memory.

At Arreton too, it seems, there is sometimes seen a silver-grey figure, possibly a monk or an abbot, for associated with this quiet shade is the sweet smell of incense, especially in the charming room just off the Great Hall. Once two people, complete strangers to each other, separately asked the owner, Count Slade de Pomeroy, whether he could account for the overwhelming smell of incense in that lovely, peaceful room. The count merely smiled, for he is used to such enquiries. It would not be the first time if he was awakened in the middle of the night by rappings on his bedroom door. Now, he ignores them. There is never anybody there. Once he was pushed in the back by something invisible to him but Mrs Welstead, who was present at the time, told him not to worry, 'two monks just came through and one of them bumped into you...'

In September 1980 Mr L.N. Welch of Eastleigh told me about a visit that he and his wife paid to Arreton Manor in June 1979. He writes: 'My wife and I had been looking round some of the splendid rooms and we reached the top of the main staircase, where there is a landing and a small room leading off to the left and a larger one to the right. My wife at this time had no knowledge of any ghostly stories associated with the house. Suddenly my wife said she was feeling distinctly uncomfortable; we entered the small room and there my wife started to turn pale and said she felt so strange she did not think she could stay in the room. She said she did not like the room and she had a strong sense of fear, almost as though someone was watching her closely and did not want her there. When we left and went into the larger room opposite, she said she had the same feeling but it was not as strong and not as bad. When we eventually came downstairs and mentioned to the receptionist the effect that the rooms had had on my wife, she told us that many people who go into the small room report a similar experience and also in the larger room, but it is not usually as bad there.

'The Count told us that when he and a relative were making up some of the exhibits in the small room, they had to keep coming down after a short while before continuing the work because they also had this strong and frightening feeling of being watched. Later I learned that on the landing between the two rooms two older brothers of Barnaby Leigh, James and Thomas, fought a duel over who should own the property; the fight ended with a sword-thrust through the heart of one brother and the other died from his wounds three days later. The small room is said to be the one from which Annabelle was thrown to her death.'

In September 1980 Count Slade de Pomeroy informed me that he had recently seen the ghost monk. He and his housekeeper saw, 'very plainly' the figure of the monk, 'twice within about thirty seconds'. It was the first and only time that he has seen a ghost at Arreton or elsewhere. Most of the ghosts of Arreton Manor seem to be gentle, gracious, quiet and peaceful memories of long ago but just occasionally something of the tragedy and violence that has occurred at Arreton seems to return to this beautiful house.

ASHEY DOWN NEAR BRADING, ISLE OF WIGHT

Here on January night in 1969, Dr White and his wife found themselves in the middle of a fantastic mystery; a unique experience that has no logical explanation. Mrs Sheila White was kind enough to tell me all about it is a letter in February 1973 and she wrote up the experience herself in an article published in the magazine Hampshire.

The late Dr White and his wife left their home at St Helens on the west coast to have dinner with some friends at Niton in the extreme south of the island. It was almost dark but a full moon shone through the cloud-filled sky as they made their unhurried and relaxed journey with the pleasant prospect of a meal with their friends. They were in a hurry and decided to take the road up over the Downs and as they reached Ashey Down they found themselves in the middle of the biggest mystery of their lives.

It was Mrs White who first saw the lights. She was very puzzled because she knew they were in the middle of a lonely stretch of country with the nearest farm houses several miles away, yet bobbing about in the fields she saw numerous flickering lights... She drew her husband's attention to them but he said it must be farmers looking for sheep or something of the sort and, for the moment, they left it at that. Then at the bottom of the steep hill to Mersley Down they were both astonished to see lights blazing in the fields on their right, so many that it looked like a town!

They stopped the car and sat looking at the hundreds of sparkling, twinkling lights spread out below them. Could it be some exhibition or event that they had not heard of? But so many lights...

Halfway up Mersley Down there is a narrow road leading to the right, where a signpost points the way to Havenstreet. They remembered the road as little more than a cart track but this night it seemed to have become a proper road, with street-lamps on either side, leading up to what appeared to be a built-up area of buildings that simply blazed with lights: red, green, orange and white. Something was going on. They looked up at the sky where black clouds scurried over the moon...

Puzzled and determined to find out what was happening they drove down the hill, past the turning to Newchurch and up the downland road towards the signpost and the cart track; by the time they arrived there was not a single light to be seen anywhere!

Completely puzzled by this time, Dr White and his wife stopped the car and got out. Everything was still and quiet and there was no sign of the great conglomeration of lights that they had both seen so plainly only moments before. Beginning to feel a little frightened and anxious to see a familiar landmark, they got back into the car and drove towards the Hare and Hounds, a well-known and fondly-regarded, cosy little thatched inn where the roads divide.

They turned the corner, looking forward to a drink and a chat about their strange experiences with the friendly landlord but suddenly they were back again in time — or whatever had happened to them. There in front of them was not the quiet inn which they knew and loved; instead it seemed to be bathed in light and scores of people were running back and forth across the road carrying torches... To their right, the fields were again filled with flickering lights... Dr White decided to stop and see whether he could find out what was happening. As he was about to do so a man, unusually tall he seemed and wearing a long jerkin and a wide leather belt, came straight towards them, although he didn't seem to see them, and then he literally passed through the front of their car! They pulled up sharply but there was no sensation of having touched anything and they began to go forward again, slowly, towards the Hare and Hounds — and when they were no more than twenty yards away, all the lights suddenly vanished. It was just as though someone had thrown a switch, Mrs White told me.

Somewhat shakily they got out of the car and went into the inn. Inside, everything was the same as always: solid, friendly — and the only lights were the ones that were always there. They looked across the fields, all was dark as far as they could see, not a light was to be seen.

When they reached Niton they told their friends the extraordinary story. No explanation was forthcoming and no satisfactory explanation has ever been found. Their return journey was completely uneventful. Could it have been some sort of mirage? The lights of Portsmouth, perhaps, reflected across the waters of the Solent? Or did they step back in time — or move forward? Had they seen the Roman Legions in their camps or was something that is yet to happen played out before them? Did Mrs White and her husband really see those lights? They often talked about the experience but they were never able to explain it.

In her letter to me Mrs White says: 'The story is entirely true and I have tried to tell it exactly as it happened. I am very sensitive to atmosphere... my husband, on the other hand, was quite the opposite. He was a very clever man, a brilliant doctor with an extremely practical outlook and logical brain. The events of that night shook him far more than he would admit because here was something that no one could possibly explain and he hated to feel that it was all quite beyond him!'

BASINGSTOKE

The White Hart in London road is, or was, haunted by the sound of something being rolled over gravel and it is only heard after midnight. The wife of a former licensee has described the noise as a sound that seemed to roll towards the hearer, then when it appeared to be about three feet away it would stop and roll back towards the next room; but it was never heard there. Then it would start again and repeat the performance all over again. On occasions the sound would be very loud and make sleep quite impossible. When that happened the occupants of the room would get up, put on the light and try to sleep in a chair. This happened many times to different people.

Once only, I believe, a ghostly figure has been seen at the White Hart. In December 1968 the licensee's mother-in-law was sleeping in the haunted room when she suddenly found herself wide awake, feeling very cold and apprehensive as to what was about to happen. As she raised her head from the pillow she saw a man push open the bedroom door, enter the room, and move towards the dressing room table. The figure stopped in front of the table and, raising both arms, seemed to smooth back its hair, then it turned towards the bed, smiled and disappeared out of the room, leaving the door open. Who this figure might be and what long-past event was being re-lived or re-enacted has not, so far, been discovered.

Once the sound that was usually heard in one room of the inn was apparently heard in the backyard early one morning, or a sound very much like it and, equally inexplicable. One of the inn staff reported hearing the sound of something heavy being dragged or rolled over gravel and at the same time he sensed rather than saw a presence without any definite shape or form.

BEAULIEU

In his delightful book In Search of England, the late H. V. Morton, who knew and loved Hampshire, wrote '. . .there is no place known to me in which you would be more likely to see a ghost in daylight than the ruins of Beaulieu Abbey. . . It is a quiet place, full of kind ghosts.' And so it is.

It is said that 'bad' King John's single worthy deed was the foundation of Beaulieu Abbey — and he was even blackmailed into that by a terrifying dream! In his dream the King saw himself put on trial, condemned and mercilessly flogged; so vivid was his dream that when he awoke, his body bore the marks of the lash. He thought he had angered God and he promptly released some Cistercian abbots whom he had imprisoned and began the building of the Abbey Church at Beaulieu.

Here there are ghostly monks, strange lights, the fragrance of incense, celestial singing and the sound of chanting at dead of night.

No monks have lived at Beaulieu since 1538 when the Abbey was dissolved but for many years there have been reports of ghost monks being seen in the area and especially in the vicinity of the cloisters. And the reports seem to have increased during the past fifty years.

In the 1920s a single monk appeared from time to time at Beaulieu and was seen by residents and casual visitors. Footsteps would often be heard approaching the ancient doorways and sometimes indoors, especially climbing stairs that were quite devoid of any visual form. Loud crashes and bangs would be heard, for which no cause or explanation was ever found.

It was during this period that Miss Aimee Cheshire lived for many years in a vast, oak-beamed, stone-walled room within the ruins of the old dormitory and she said she often heard footsteps and the clink of keys. It was here that the monks, four centuries before, used to sleep in cells, being awakened by one of their number in the small hours to welcome the new day with matins. Sometimes Miss Cheshire, and other people who stayed there, would hear the sound of a choir singing. This might happen at any hour of the day or night but always, it seemed, when it was least expected. On one occasion two friends came to dinner with Miss Cheshire and they were very sceptical of the sounds of monks that she told them she had heard many times. In the middle of the meal the gentle sound pervaded the whole room and all three heard it at the same time. No sooner were they fully aware of the sound than it ceased.

The Revd Robert Frazer Powles died in 1940 after spending no fewer than sixty years as curate and vicar of Beaulieu and to him the ghost monks were for years as genuine and natural as any mortal, so real and so much a part of his daily life that he quietly accepted their presence and whenever he spoke of them, which was seldom, he did so with reverence and complete conviction.

During the Second World War a sighting of the ghost monks was reported from an unexpected quarter. At the time a small anti-aircraft detachment was posted at nearby Buckler's Hard and one afternoon a couple of officers were driving past the Abbey when they saw a small group of monks in the Abbey grounds.

When they next saw the vicar who acted as their chaplain, they asked him which order the monks belonged to. The vicar told them that the Beaulieu monks had been Cistercians but there had been no monks in the Abbey since 1538. He and the puzzled officers ascertained that no real monks had visited Beaulieu on the day that they had clearly seen the figures.

A retired nurse, Mrs Samuels, who occupied a flat in the Domus Conversorum, walked out on to the little stone landing at the top of her stairway one Sunday morning and saw, seated in a recess beside a magnolia tree, the figure of a monk reading a scroll. She watched him for a few minutes and then returned indoors to make herself a cup of tea. When she returned the monk had completely vanished.

Some years ago I talked with Mr H. Widnell, a mine of information on Beaulieu, and he told me about what he liked to call 'a curious echo from the past' that always puzzled him. It concerned a lady whom Widnell knew well for many years and who lived at the time in one of the old Beaulieu houses, through which the precinct or sanctuary wall runs.

This lady had a curiously vivid dream — or possibly a vision, she was never sure herself — in which a man came into the hall one evening and when she asked him what he wanted, he told her that he had killed a man in the wood, had cut off the head and the right hand, as it was mutilated, and had buried them outside the precinct wall and now he wanted them buried in sanctified ground. He intimated that digging at a spot he specified would reveal the human remains and also two stones, one of which she was to 'give to the Abbot' and the other she was to keep for herself. Here there are variations in the story, one version stating that digging was duly carried out and the bones recovered and reburied together with the two stones that were also found as foretold. But Widnell always maintained that a concrete floor was laid where the bones were supposed to be buried and no digging in fact took place. What did happen was that noises — footsteps, bangs and crashing sounds — and the reappearance of the phantom man, so troubled the lady concerned that she consulted my informant who happened to know Sir Arthur Conan Doyle (who was then living at nearby Lyndhurst) and his great interest in such matters and the outcome was that Sir Arthur and Lady Conan Doyle, another couple and the lady and Wignall all met and held a seance in the drawing room on the sanctuary side of the precinct wall.

I relate the rest of the story in H. Widnell's own words— 'Sir Arthur, who was the most reverent of men, as well as the most earnest in such matters, began with a prayer, and then inquired if there were a spirit which haunted the house, at which the table spelt out 'yes'. Sir Arthur asked next whether the spirit was troubled, or earth- bound and wished to be freed? In each case the answer was in the affirmative. Sir Arthur then requested the spirit to tell his former name, whereat the unusual name of 'de Ceigunal' was spelt out. After this Sir Arthur addressed the spirit, commanding it not to be troubled any more and to depart in peace.

'As to whether the spirit was actually contacted by Sir Arthur and his circle, there are others better able to judge than the writer. It can, however, be affirmed in the most definite manner possible, that the proceedings were conducted from beginning to end with the utmost seriousness and gravity. Undoubtedly too the footsteps and noises began to decrease.'

I may say that Wignall was always strangely reluctant to talk about the ghosts of Beaulieu although he wrote about them in his contribution to a volume entitled The New Forest, edited by the Earl of Radnor in 1960. In 1967 I asked Widnall whether he would like to address members of the Ghost Club on the subject and I quote his reply dated 12 November 1967, from Abbeymead, Beaulieu, the last time I heard from him:

'. . .You have paid me a very kind compliment and one which I much appreciate. I am afraid however that I cannot accept your offer to give a talk for two reasons; firstly, I shall not be in London on January 1st, and secondly, I am reluctant to talk of these 'matters' too freely. I have a strong feeling that my 'subjects' think that I am rather exploiting them and object accordingly. I was hesitant to write what I did but was especially asked to do so, and my reluctance increased after I had agreed to the request. I am sure that as one keenly interested in these 'affairs' you will understand my feelings. With again many thanks for having been so kind as to ask me...'

In 1965 I went to see Diana Norman (wife of the television film authority Barry Norman) when her book *The Stately Ghosts of England* had just appeared in which she visited a dozen haunted stately houses in the company of my old friend, clairvoyant Tom Corbett, and she told me— 'We never encountered such a mass of evidence from one stately home as we encountered at Beaulieu.' Lord Montagu told her, as he told me when I visited beautiful Beaulieu, 'You'll find ghosts are part of the scene here.' He told me he had never seen any of the ghosts but he fully accepted that the place was haunted. He has experienced the strong smell of incense that so many people have reported.

One night, entertaining some guests to dinner in his dining room, formerly the Gatehouse Upper Chapel, a sudden and very strong smell of incense wafted through the room. Everyone was aware of it — but that was not an uncommon occurrence at Beaulieu, I was told.

Colonel Robert Gore-Browne lived in an isolated house on the estate and he saw a ghost monk one evening at dusk as he was walking his dog along the lane that passed his house. Some way ahead and walking towards him, he saw a figure in brown with the skirt brushing the ground. At first he thought it was a woman and he prepared to have a word with whoever it might be. He went down a small dip and then up again, but when he reached the brow of the little hill there was nobody in sight. He looked carefully on either side of the path but there was no trace of the figure he had seen. The dog showed no sign of being aware of anything unusual. 'It may have been a ghost,' said the Colonel afterwards. 'It may not — but some funny things do go on around here... that's for certain.'

When they first came to Beaulieu the Gore-Brownes had a Swiss parlourmaid and she always said she saw a ghost. One night she was late going up to her room and switched on the passage light to see her way. When she opened her bedroom door the light from the passage shone in and she saw a man lying on the sofa in her room. By the time she had fetched someone the figure had disappeared but she described the form she had seen in great detail — a bright red face with white whiskers. Some time later they met a man whose uncle had lived in the house: he had a bright red face and white whiskers.

When I was at Beaulieu I talked with Michael Sedgwick, curator of the Montagu Motor Museum, who lived in a cottage on the east side of the Abbey Church. He told me that he had twice heard the sound of chanting. The first time was just before Christmas 1959, when he was particularly busy and had been working very late, typing and chain-smoking as he did so. At length he decided to open the windows and let some clean air into the room before he went to bed. As he opened the window he heard distinct and definite chanting. It was very beautiful but came in uneven waves, not unlike a faulty radio. For a moment it would be quite loud and then suddenly it would fade away, almost completely, and then return again, clear and distinct.

The second time Michael had heard the chanting he had again been up very late working and he heard the same sounds, again fading and then coming back, several times as he opened the window. On each occasion he had noticed that it had been a still, crisp night.

One of Beaulieu's catering manageresses heard similar sounds late one night just before another Christmas. It sounded to her almost like a service being held in the church — beautiful singing, 'something to be remembered for always.'

Mrs McMurtrie, wife of Group Captain R.A. McMurtrie, lived in Palace Lane cottage at Beaulieu in the early 1930s and she told my friend, Air Commodore R.C. Jonas about her experiences when they met in Washington, D.C., in December 1948. They had experienced the unmistakable and inexplicable sound of footsteps, time after time. Doors had opened and closed by themselves, times without number. They had both heard the sound of whispering voices and other odd sounds and although Mrs McMurtrie remained convinced that most if not all the sounds could be explained by natural causes, these causes were never found and previous and subsequent occupants of the house reported hearing the same seemingly inexplicable sounds.

On the north-east side of the church there is a plot of ground which is believed to have been the place where the monks buried their dead. Here, especially at night, slow and ponderous footsteps have been heard, as though something heavy is being carried. It is possible to watch the progress of the noise as it moves — and it even sounds different when it crosses a bridge over a stream, I have been told by those who have heard it. The series of sounds ends with a thump and the sound of earth being shovelled but nothing is visible.

The haunted stream at Bramshott

As recently as August 1980 I received a report of strange happenings at Beaulieu. It came from Paul Sangster of Bognor Regis and detailed a night he and two friends spent at Beaulieu on 4 August, 1979. That night, he tells me, was clear and cold with a rising moon. The party took up their positions on the east side of the Cloister at 8.58 p.m. and all was quiet and there was nothing to report until 12.15 a.m. The watchers took turns for one of their party to rest for an hour every three hours. At exactly 2.15 a.m. the two on watch saw seven points of light moving from north to south across the centre of the Cloister. A photograph was immediately taken and this shows quite clearly two groups of three lights followed by a single one. It has been suggested that the monks could have been holding a Mass at this time and were on their way there. Dawn broke at 4.30 a.m. At 5.03 a.m. the two watchers on duty saw a shadowy figure in the area of the gateway to the lane on the west side of the Cloisters, directly facing them. This figure appeared to turn towards the north or his left, and then back towards the watchers before turning the same way again, then with its back towards the watchers it appeared to take two or three steps before fading from sight. On immediately walking over to the spot where the figure had disappeared the investigators discovered that the temperature there was ten degrees colder than on the other side of the Cloisters. The whole sighting of the monk, if monk it was, lasted, I am told 'a good five minutes' but photographs taken with and without flash on two cameras revealed no figure.

Do the monks of Beaulieu still walk? It would seem that there is evidence to suggest that they do but, as Lord Montagu once said to me, 'The ghosts here have never been evil; in fact I don't think they have ever been anything but extremely friendly but they have been seen and heard by countless people...'

BENTLEY

The author's house in Bentley

A ghost has been seen, twice by different people, in my own home and I have yet to see her, but she would seem to be a gentle shade, glimpsed very rarely; a quiet ghost who haunts the house where once she lived. Once a man who had never been to the house before saw her and described her as a short, dumpy, Victorian lady, standing with her arms crossed and smiling beside a door that leads to the stairs. A few months later another visitor, a young lady who had never been to the house before and knew nothing about the previous sighting, said, as she was about to leave, that she thought there was a ghost standing by the door leading to the stairs; a short Victorian lady who seemed to be smiling, with folded arms. Subsequently my wife caught a glimpse of a small arm with a white sleeve that appeared near the same spot.

Perhaps the best-known haunted house in Bentley is Jenkyn Place, one of the oldest houses in the parish. When I took a party of Ghost Club members to Jenkyn Place in July 1980, the delightful owner for the last forty years, Gerald Coke, CBE, JP, DL, told us something of the history of the house and its justly-famous beautiful garden and he told us, modestly, 'I suppose you could call this a haunted house'.

An early seventeenth century mellow English country house of great character and charm, Jenkyn Place apparently harbours several ghosts. One of the most persistent is known as 'Mrs Waggs' although who she is or was nobody knows. Perhaps a former housekeeper or possibly a children's nurse. There could have been many such people in the long history of the house. It seems likely that there were buildings on the site for centuries, probably long before 1687 when Robert and Ann Lutman built the farm, which forms the core of the present house that today stands only a few yards from the lane but is almost invisible until you reach the forecourt.

Somewhere in the garden — described to me by a member of the Royal Horticultural Society as one of the most beautiful gardens he had ever seen — or possibly under the present house, is Jancknes's Well which is mentioned in Domesday Book. The Pilgrims' Way passed over what is now the front drive of Jenkyn Place and pilgrims, on their way from Froyle Church to Bentley Church, are reputed to have paused to drink at the well and throw in a coin for luck!

Jenkyn Place

Long before the Cokes came to Jenkyn Place, during the occupancy of the Lawsons, back in the 1920s, the haunting seems to have been well-established and varied. There was the unidentified White Lady who walked across the little bridge over the lane; a frequently reported apparition that is well remembered by some of the villagers today. There was the strangely brilliant but quite inexplicable light that was often seen in a little upper window, a light that invariably extinguished itself whenever anyone sought to make an investigation and a light that was seen whether or not any of the occupants of Jenkyn Place were at home. And there was the phantom coach-and-horses. An unusual wealth of evidence would appear to exist for this arresting manifestation. That mine of information about ghosts of the Farnham area, my good friend Dorothea St Hill Bourne tells me that she located eight first hand witnesses for the phantom coach which used to drive over the cross-roads at Bentley and draw up at Jenkyn Place. And I have talked with a former employee of the Lawsons who well remembers talking to more than one reliable person who claimed to have seen the phantom coach; one was his own brother who, more than fifty years later, still maintains that he saw and heard this remarkable phenomenon and that there was no natural explanations that could account for the experience.

The anonymous Mrs Waggs has been seen many times at Jenkyn Place during the last hundred years and usually during the winter months. She has been seen in the hall (significantly perhaps, part of the older structure), on the stairs that run up the west side of the house and in an upstairs sitting room, my wife and I were told when Mr and Mrs Coke very kindly showed us over the house a few years ago.

There is a tradition that the figure disappears into a second room at the head of the stairs, picks up a lighted candle and then continues her tour of the upper part of the house. The bedroom which the ghost reputedly visits has three heart-shaped pieces of wood inserted into the flooring to replace knots in the wood and a formidable iron bar on the inside of the door that looks as though it could hold the door fast against anything in the world, but whether these features have any connection with the ghost or the haunting is not known. The bar is ingeniously constructed and there was once a rope running to the wall by the bed so that the door could be fastened as required by someone while they were in bed...

At the top of the stairs there is a curious space between age-old beams and here something very horrible is supposed to have happened in the eighteenth century, or possibly a little later; something so horrible that the details were never revealed but within living memory one visitor encountered 'something' at this spot which they would never talk about.

On the south side of the house one of the sons of the present owner saw a female figure when he was a boy of six or seven. He was very shaken by the experience and told his mother that he had seen a woman dressed like a housekeeper pass through his bedroom. In this part of the house we were shown a door that used continuously to open by itself. At one time the door became such a nuisance with its incessant opening, no matter how often or how firmly it was closed, that a spring was fitted so now the door closes by itself instead of opening by itself!

On the west side of the house there is a most charming little bedroom that was allocated not very long ago to a sensible eighteen-year-old friend of the family during her visit to Jenkyn Place. She spent one night in the room and said she could not possibly sleep there again. She gave no real reason for her discomfort and was not pressed by the family for details.

Some years ago John Christie, founder of the Glyndebourne Festival and holder of the Military Cross, visited Jenkyn Place (Gerald Coke was Chairman of Glyndebourne Arts Trust from 1955 to 1975) and he was taking tea in the upstairs sitting room when he suddenly remarked upon the fact that a housekeeper who had been standing between the settee and the door, had seemed to disappear into the wall! He had no knowledge of the reputed ghost but if the figure had passed through the wall at the place he indicated this would have led to the spot where the ghost is traditionally reputed to be seen.

What would appear to be the same figure has been seen by other visitors and by local people who all say that she is dressed in a fitting mob- cap, brown dress, white apron with the ends turned up and many witnesses find the figure reminiscent of the Jane Austen period.

Members of the Joy family, a well-known local family, have seen the ghost at Jenkyn Place. Where I was at 'Marelands' in September 1980, Michael Joy told me that one winter day during the Second World War, when Jenkyn Place was empty, he and his mother, an aunt and two of his sisters were shown over the house by a caretaker. Michael Joy, his aunt and one of his sisters had remained in one of the downstairs rooms while his mother and another sister were taken off by the caretaker to another part of the house.

After a little while the three thought they had better catch up with the rest of the party but they did not know where the caretaker had gone. They stood in the hall and saw the figure of a woman near the top of the stairs; she walked away from them and disappeared through a door. Naturally they thought they had seen the caretaker and they hastily followed up the stairs but when they reached the top they heard the caretaker's voice downstairs and she appeared with old Mrs Joy and one of her grandchildren. There was nobody other than themselves upstairs and nobody else in the house at the time. The Aunt, Miss Phyllis Joy, described the figure as a 'little old woman in black'.

Other unidentified ghosts at Bentley include the white form that reputedly haunts the churchyard with its enormous and awesome yew trees that may well be as old as the church that probably dates from 1170, the year of the murder of Thomas a Becket in Canterbury Cathedral. It is possible to speculate indefinitely on the possible identity and origin of the fleeting figure in the dark churchyard where some long-forgotten incident may have left its mark for ever.

As we have seen a phantom coach-and-horses has long been reputed to haunt Bentley crossroads and there is a ghost monk that occasionally crosses the A31 not far from the drive that leads to the old oast-house. Not long ago a resident told me that she distinctly saw the figure of a monk hurrying along the roadway one bright moonlit night but by the time she crossed the road the figure had completely and inexplicably disappeared. The level-headed farmer's wife found that she was terrified although she didn't really know why and now she avoids that stretch of the road as much as she can on moonlit nights.

Incidentally the phantom coach story was confirmed by, among others, Mrs Tomkins who lived at Bay Tree Cottage; she said she had heard and seen the coach on more than one occasion. Once the owner of a cottage near the crossroads was sitting in the garden one evening when she heard the grind of wheels and rattle of harness but when she looked there was nothing to be seen and the sounds ceased.

Then there is a ghost dog that the occupants of a house near the church used to see from their windows but the animal had always disappeared by the time one was outside the house. It was unlike any local dog and various members of the family saw the dog many times; it was also seen by visitors, but after the house changed hands the phantom dog was never seen again. It seems there is another animal ghost at Bentley, a dog-like creature that crosses the road not far from the village shop. And there is sombre and solid Marsh House where a former inhabitant was repeatedly disturbed by a sound like the beating of wings in one of the bedrooms. . . while nearby the Bull Inn has been the scene of some strange happenings. A previous licensee told me that he repeatedly saw the figure of a short, dark man in the vicinity of the fireplace in the small bar at the time that efforts were being made to restore the fireplace to its original form. Unexplained footsteps have been heard in various parts of the old inn over the years and the last licensee related to me many little incidents that he could not explain, from articles moving, disappearing and reappearing in odd places to forms of people and animals glimpsed, just for a second, in some dark corner of the hostelry or its garden. The present delightful occupants, Peter and Mary Holmes, are constantly aware of odd happenings, lights being unaccountably switched off or on, the heating apparatus being interfered with, footsteps and other noises for which no explanation is ever forthcoming, but they have learned to live with these minor irritations and have succeeded in making The Bull a happy place to foregather for local people and passing trade.

The house now known as Fox Hall was once a farm owned by nearby Waverley Abbey and ghost monks are said to have been seen in the garden at Fox Hall and in an adjoining garden. There was also the ghost of an old man who used to walk round the house at twilight. A priest stayed at the Hall on one occasion and saw the ghost. When he was told that the ghost walked most evenings, the priest said, 'You can't let the poor old man go walking round the house like that for ever' and he made a point of encountering the apparition. When he did so he administered absolution and the ghost was not seen again!

Fox Hall

Originally Fox Hall was called 'Allynes' and Bonnie Prince Charlie is said to have slept there while on a secret visit to England. Certainly he is known to have been at Godalming ten miles away, and until about fifty years ago a hat was preserved at the Hall that was said to have belonged to the Prince.

Marelands is a beautiful old house, full of atmosphere, rare charm and delightful rooms. It has a splendid view over the Wey Valley, both from the south front of the house and from the charming Long Terrace. The property has been much altered over the years; its various owners and occupants have often been individual characters and, by all accounts, it was at one time very haunted.

Marelands

In 1942 the late Christopher Hussey (whose home Scotney Castle in Kent is itself haunted) wrote in *Country Life* about Marelands, then the home of Mrs Douglas Joy and still, at the time of writing, the home of one of her descendants. Christopher Hussey felt that it was a house of memories, some charming, some sinister; and as my wife and I walked through the utterly delightful rooms and corridors and stairways in September 1980, we too felt something of the people who had once lived there and of the peace and tranquillity that only seems to be found in old houses that have been loved for centuries; and yet there is a haunted room...

There are old references to Marelands as early as the fourteenth century when it was known as Merschcopemed (a meadow sloping down to a marsh); and a little later it is referred to as la Merre; early in the fifteenth century it is Mereland, suggesting a lake or mere and from there it was only a step to the present name. Much of the west part of the house is Georgian, while the shorter centre part is certainly a lot older with its charming 'Chinese Chippendale' porch added about 1750. The fine marble chimneypiece, decorated with a medallion of Medusa's head, to be seen in the octagon, once the dining-room, was probably put there by one 'individual' owner, the 'wicked' Lord Stawell.

We know that Gilbert White's brother Benjamin was at Marelands in 1793 when the old man of Selborne stayed with his brother and indeed, in 1918, during the course of structural alterations, one of Gilbert White's visiting cards was found under the dining-room floor. It was replaced where it had been found because old Hampshire folk say it is unlucky to take a thing away from the place where you find it.

Previously the house seems to have belonged to Lord Sawell and his agent, a Mr Salisbury, apparently resided there, a man who reportedly 'dropped suddenly out of his chair and was dead in a moment, on the eve of his birthday, while his wife was preparing an elegant entertainment for his friends the day following...

Tradition has long associated Lord Stawell with the murder of an illegitimate child, but it seems likely that the very similar stories told about Marelands and Hinton Ampner, both homes of Lord

Stawell, have become confused over the years. One story tells of Lord Stawell himself murdering the child he had by a housekeeper at Marelands and burying it beneath a hearthstone; another version has it that his agent or steward (Mr Salisbury perhaps) carried out the dastardly deed in one of the bedrooms. At all events in 1918 'the calcinated bones of a child were found beneath the hearthstone in one of the ground floor rooms.'

Perhaps the bedroom in which the murder took place was the room that became the 'haunted room', a bedroom on the west side of Marelands which has an unusual domed ceiling and a very curious atmosphere.

When my friend Dorothea St Hill Bourne visited Marelands in 1963, she and her sister felt the picturesque but rather 'queer' staircase to be haunted and the 'haunted room' she thought to be 'distinctly haunted'. This is where, according to the late Miss Phyllis Joy, who once lived at Marelands, 'things' had been seen by various people sleeping in the haunted room. She used to say 'Marelands is very haunted and has a dreadful feeling'. This same Miss Joy had once felt a 'cold and clammy hand' on her shoulder as she walked up the stairs at Marelands. On the other hand Michael Joy, the present owner, has never seen or heard a ghost at Marelands and does not feel the house to be haunted. He told us that the so-called 'haunted room' had been used times without number by visitors, young and old, and he had never heard that their rest had been disturbed in any way.

Miss Phyllis Joy, however, believed that this was the room there the murder had been committed by the 'wicked Lord Stawell' and that he had haunted the house for many years, until in fact a service of exorcism had been held in the house during the days of old Mrs Douglas Joy, who went to Marelands in 1918, where she lived on into the 1950s and was over ninety when she died.

At one time there was talk of an everlasting bloodstain on one of the hearthstones and of a pond in the grounds being haunted by someone who had committed suicide. There were also stories of Henry, Lord Stawell 'dabbling' in Black Magic and keeping an assortment of strange beasts for strange practices at Marelands but most of these tales seem to have little basis in fact and my wife and I found Marelands a sombre, charming, lovingly cared-for and peaceful house, full of memories and brooding quietly amid the lush meadows. I don't think I agree with Dorothea St Hill Bourne who once said, after visiting the house, 'While the whole place is charming to look at, it has a sinister feeling even in bright daylight...' Perhaps it is a case of the eye of the beholder!

BISHOPS WALTHAM

A few years ago my wife and I visited several times a lovely old house in Saint Peter's Street where footsteps were repeatedly heard walking up the stairs; where a dark figure had been seen in various parts of the house and where strange noises seemed to follow one of the inhabitants.

At the request of the inhabitants I took a medium there and he thought that two huge native carvings had something to do with the disturbances. A singular aspect of the case was the terrifying fact that all four of the children had been repeatedly taken seriously ill and seemingly near to death's door, were saved only by urgent medical attention; although before coming to live at this lovely old house they had all been Healthy and hardy. Even the family doctor was very puzzled as to why so many serious afflictions should foist themselves on one family in such a short space of time. At least one of the occupants had no doubt about the reason: the house was haunted.

I made a number of suggestions that I hope were helpful and I talked privately and individually with the two adult members of the household and since I heard no more, I like to think that everything sorted itself out, but sometimes I wonder, for there was a very strange atmosphere pervading the house on the three occasions that I visited the elegant and utterly charming house.

I did learn that the massive native idols had come from Africa and there had been some violent dispute about their possession and removal with threats of retribution by some powerful and evil means, but this could not have anything to do with the odd events at the house — or could it?

BISHOPSTOKE

In 1972 and 1973 I spent several hours on several occasions at a house in Nelson Road where the occupants, a man and his wife and two small children, seemed to be living in a world of fear.

It had all begun nearly two years earlier, and the first incident, as with so many cases of apparent haunting, was perhaps the least difficult to explain. A large glass bowl was found moved from its accustomed place on a window-sill of one room and placed in an armchair in another room, in the time it took to enter the house.

After that several similar incidents took place and it began to dawn on the occupants that something very odd was happening. No one was breaking into the house. It seemed impossible for any of the occupants to be responsible. On occasions considerable force was employed — once a washing machine was moved and once the bathroom taps were screwed down so tightly that a spanner was required to unscrew them. Reluctantly they came to the conclusion that their previously happy home was possessed of a restless spirit.

Investigation into the previous history of the house revealed that the property had once been occupied by a middle-aged couple, and before that by an elderly couple who had lived there for many years and who had eventually both been killed in a car accident while returning home from a visit to friends. The young couple became convinced that this couple who had met such a tragic and violent end were haunting their old home.

They went to see a minister who introduced them to another clergyman who promised to visit the house and see what he could do. By this time things were getting worse. The much-loved family cat was found shut fast in a linen box with a bowl of heavy wet washing placed on top. The pet white rabbit was 'transported' from the outside shed to the sideboard drawer — where she chewed through half-a-dozen tablecloths and ate up some insurance policies before she was found. A guinea pig was taken out of its cage and killed in the garden. It was found one morning, still warm, its eyes wide open, no bones crushed, no blood anywhere, but very dead.

The clergyman who had been recommended duly arrived. He said he was experienced in laying unquiet spirits to rest and he made a tour of the whole house with a divining rod. Some rooms he found so badly haunted that he was nearly physically sick. He said there were two ghosts and he indicated where they were standing at that moment— one on each side of the fireplace, watching and listening. He said they were not dangerous and promised to return and carry out a service of exorcism.

Meanwhile the disturbing events continued. Cooking utensils would disappear; wrist watches would be moved; spectacles would be lost and found in odd places. There were literally hundreds of such incidents, I was told. And always the occupants of that ordinary little house felt that they were being watched and listened to, wherever they were and whatever they were doing, and gradually they came to feel afraid.

Then came the touchings. At odd moments and when they least expected it, they would feel a sensation of fingers: the strings of an apron would be tugged, a back would be touched, an ankle would be grasped for a second; always when no one else was in the room. Once a punch in the face knocked one of the adults from an armchair to the floor near the fireplace.

One of the little girls would wake up and say she heard whispering or that she could feel a weight on the bed, as though somebody were sitting on her legs. Soon these experiences distressed her so much that she would cry and scream and it seemed that she could never be left alone at night.

The clergyman duly returned and carried out his service of exorcism and he explained that the elderly couple were unable to resign themselves to death and could not understand why there were other people in their house. He filled the rooms with the smell of herbs and incense and spices; he prayed and asked for peace and rest; he sprinkled holy water. Immediately an overwhelming stench of manure filled the room but the reverend gentleman said this was quite common and due to the effect of the spirit departing from the house. He said he had sensed a presence following him through the house and he had cornered it in the last room and since there was no unexorcised part of the interior of the house, it had escaped by the front door, leaving its smell as it departed.

Thankful that their troubles were at last over, the young man and his wife saw the clergyman to his car, thanked him for his help, and returned to the house — where they were met by the sight of a bowl of sugar turned upside down in the armchair where the clergyman had been sitting...

Back came the clergyman and he talked with the children. He spoke to each in turn, holding their hands, and then he wielded a pendulum over their open palms. It should have revolved to denote male or female but over the palm of one little girl and over the palm of her father, it remained stationary. The clergyman believed that this indicated that these two individuals possessed mediumistic powers and while he remained convinced that he had laid one of the spirits to rest, he thought that the other was able to continue to exist, through the mediums resident in the house. He carried out another service of exorcism and said the place was free of all un-terrestrial beings and there would be no further trouble.

But it was not to be. Things continued much as before and the family borrowed a relative's dog in the hope that it might keep the bad forces at bay or give warning when something was about to happen. Instead, the dog was driven nearly mad as it frantically and repeatedly tried to get out of the house during the daytime and whimpered and howled all night. Eventually the animal became dangerous and had to be destroyed.

By this time there was hardly a movable object in the house that had not been interfered with by some unknown force. Once when I was there a shoe mysteriously appeared inside a bed, tucked right down among the bedclothes. Moments before it had been standing with its partner neatly beside the bed. Things became so bad that none of the occupants could bear to be alone in the house for fear of what might happen. The last straw was the discovery of a carving knife in one of the girl's beds. Luckily it was found before the child went to bed but as soon as it was placed on a table, it moved again — and then a second time; for a long time they looked for it and eventually found it inside a record-player!

Scores of small articles disappeared and were never found: combs, clocks, toothpaste, grocery items — and always there was a lowering of temperature around the time that anything happened. I hoped that I helped with one or two visits and one or two suggestions. I think perhaps I did because they promised to let me know of any further developments and I heard no more.

BRADING, ISLE OF WIGHT

Osborn-Smith Wax Museum

Age is the thing about Brading. Perhaps the High Street is not as picturesque as it might be with its jumbled collection of shops and public houses and cottages but it has a church eight hundred years old, the remains of a house twice that age and antiquarians will tell you that the narrow road near the church, leading past the vicarage to the old quay, was used by the Phoenicians who came here four thousand years ago. Relics of past times are everywhere: the village stocks and whipping post at the little town hall; a bull ring at the top of the hill — twelve burial mounds of Bronze Age Britons; and, perhaps above all, the splendid Roman villa discovered by shepherds in 1880.

At the top of the High Street, difficult to miss in fact, is the Osborne-Smith Wax Museum, ablaze with light and full of history. The original structure was built around 1499, on the site of a considerably older building but what this building was is a matter of conjecture. Certainly in the last five hundred years the premises have been a Guild House, brew house, bawdy inn, a cottage — and for a very long time the place has been haunted.

Long ago when the Inn was here, back in the days when the sea came into what is now Brading marsh and the town was a sizeable seaport, these rooms would be full of seamen, gamblers, prostitutes, thieves and every kind of riff-raff. It was to the Crown Inn, so goes the story, that a Frenchman came, one Louis de Rochefort, a gentleman certainly although what business he had in Brading no one knew then and no one knows now. Possibly he was an emissary from the King of France, carrying a message for Charles I, imprisoned in Carisbrooke Castle; perhaps he was a prosperous traveller on some lawful business.

At all events it seems that he dined well and was shown to an upstairs room overlooking Quay Lane where he undressed, went to bed and was soon asleep. Soon a shadowy figure crept into de Rochefort's room, a figure with an open knife clutched in his hand! Suddenly the figure sprang at the dark, sleeping figure, the knife plunged downwards once, twice, three times... de Rochefort's dying screams echoed through the house and the murderer fled. Was he an assassin hired by Cromwell? No one knows but today the murder is vividly and realistically recalled by a display in the Wax Museum. The murderer closing the heavy door with bloodstained hands, the victim sinking back on to the bed, the knife protruding from his chest... but in reality, so runs the story, with his dying breath the Frenchman cursed his murderer and swore to haunt the building until his remains were returned to his homeland and buried in his native soil.

All down the centuries there have been reports of the Frenchman haunting the old inn, succeeding premises, residential cottages, still the haunting persists, the ghost walking the creaking boards of the old building waiting for retribution. Generations of occupants followed one another and still the haunt continued. For more than a century the house was owned by a family named Carlet, one after the other they told of strange noises, inexplicable manifestations, the occasional glimpse of a tall, aristocratic figure in one of the bedrooms overlooking Quay Lane... screams shatter the quiet of the night, the clatter of an invisible coach rattles down the lane outside the house...

As recently as just a few years ago, according to Evan Lightfoot, writing in December 1973, neighbours saw the transparent form of a tall, thin man gliding along the balcony. Appearances of the ghost of Louis de Rochefort are said to have caused the last tenant of the house to move out in a hurry. And dogs almost invariably seem to be aware of 'something' on the first floor.

In 1964, while digging to install a main waterpipe, workmen discovered a human skeleton. Could this be the remains of Louis de Rochefort, come to light at last? Mr Graham Osborn-Smith decided to send the bones to France and arrange for Christian burial but no descendants of the mysterious Frenchman could be traced in his home town of Rochefort and the skeleton was brought back to Brading and is now exhibited in the museum. Poor 'Lonely Louis' (as the museum staff call him) seems doomed to walk the house for ever

A far more pleasant ghost haunts another house in Brading. When potter Krystyna Young had her pottery in a building that had once been an old coaching inn, she often heard what sounded like pattering footsteps, light and gentle but quite inexplicable and not really frightening. Often the sounds would be heard around three o'clock in the afternoon, more or less throughout the year and usually they sounded as though from a room above, although Mrs Young would often be completely alone in the old premises. Just once a little girl who stayed with the Youngs was frightened at sleeping in the room where the footsteps most frequently seemed to originate. Some of the girls who worked for Mrs Young at the pottery heard the sounds too and everyone seemed to agree that they sounded like the footsteps of a child.

When the Youngs left the new owners seemed to

inherit the ghost and they reported a year or two ago that in addition to the daytime footsteps they heard also the sound of a door opening and closing and sometimes they heard sounds at night that they were at a complete loss to explain.

BRAMSHILL NEAR READING

You see imposing red-bricked Bramshill far away at the end of the mile-long straight drive and as you slowly approach, the graceful and mellow building comes into perfect perspective: the gabled roof, the mullioned windows, the ornate Jacobean facade... and as you arrive and climb the wide steps to the front door, guarded by two miniature cannon, you find yourself wondering whether this is the house that saw the tragic episode that became known as the Legend of the Mistletoe Bough.

Briefly, the story concerns the wedding of the beautiful daughter of the family one Christmas Eve, the mansion decked with holly and the bride carrying a sprig of mistletoe. After the ceremony and wedding breakfast the bride challenges her husband to find her in a game of hide-and-seek. The bridegroom, the family and the guests are said to have searched high and low with growing concern but hours, days, weeks later the bride had not been found. At length a servant, looking for some sheets, lifted the lid of a long-disused chest which had a lock that could only be opened Irom the outside and there inside lay the mouldering form of the once-fair bride, still clutching a sprig of mistletoe. The ghost of the girl, dressed in her white bridal gown and carrying a sprig of mistletoe, is said to have haunted her former home ever since... but let us look for a moment at the documented history of this lovely house.

Bramshill House

Bramshill or Bromeselle as it was known in Saxon times (references to the house can be traced back to the days of Edward the Confessor) is twice mentioned in Domesday Book (1086) where the great Hugh de Port is named as owner and described as 'a Leviathan of Hampshire landholders and indeed the Norman family held the lordship of the manor for nine generations by which time their name had been changed to St John of Basing. From the St Johns the property passed to Sir John Foxley who built a chapel and enclosed thousands acres of land which he laid down as a deer park and, perhaps, built the original mansion on the 'Hill of Broom'. When I was at Bramshill in August 1980 the massive 'Foxley Door' was pointed out to me — what stories it could tell if only it could talk... An ancient gateway and part of the cellars are all that now remain of the fourteenth century building.

Foxley was Constable of Windsor Castle and in charge of reconstruction work then being carried out at the royal residence and there is speculation that he introduced into the architecture of Bramshill some of the ideas and designs executed at Windsor.

There is something interesting about each of the successive owners of this fascinating house. In 1489 the mansion came into the possession of Elizabeth Essex, the thirteen-year-old heiress of her father Thomas Rogers, and her husband William Essex aged twelve; the couple had already been married for two years. They were at Bramshill for ten years until, in 1399, Henry VII's chamberlain, Lord Daubeney, acquired the property. Forty-eight years later the manor and its broad acres reverted to the St Johns of Basing whose family had been raised to the peerage by Henry VIII. Lord St John became the first Marquess of Winchester and he and his successors retained Branshill until 1600 when the fourth Marquess was obliged to dispose of it.

In 1605 Edward, Lord Zouche of Harringworth became lord of the manor and promptly demolished the greater part of old Bramshill and started to build the present house on the original site, using much of the old material. It was a majestic property when it was completed in 1612 with immense rooms, fine ceilings of great beauty and he adorned the walls with artistic paintings and rare tapestries. One of the very finest of Jacobean mansions, there may be some truth in the story that it was intended as a gift for Henry, Prince of Wales, eldest son of James I but the Prince died tragically, never living to see the house completed with its great Long Gallery (now used as part of the Library) twice the length of a cricket pitch and bearing comparison with any gallery in England

It was while Lord Zouche lived in his magnificent new house that an extraordinary happening took place, a tragic event that could conceivably have contributed to the atmosphere conducive to ghosts.

During the course of a visit to Bramshill the Most Reverend George Abbot, Archbishop of Canterbury, went out to shoot deer with a crossbow but shot instead a keeper on the estate. The barbed arrow pierced the keeper's arm, severing an artery, and within an hour the man was dead. Overcome with remorse and affected by the public outcry that followed the accident, the Archbishop was suspended from his office and retired into seclusion to await the verdict of an ecclesiastical enquiry. Ultimately the Archbishop was restored to his clerical position but it is said he never smiled again and certainly he did all he could to provide for the widow of the unfortunate keeper. It transpired that Lord Zouche had warned the keeper to stand well clear of His Grace, whose shooting was known to be erratic.

On the death of Lord Zouche in 1625 Bramshill passed to a kinsman who sold the estate, in 1638, to the second Earl of Antrim. Two years later it was purchased by the extravagant Sir Robert Henley whose representatives and creditors sold it, in 1699, to Sir John Cope. It remained in the Cope family for almost two hundred and fifty years, being occupied by nine successive holders of that ancient baronetcy that was created by James I in 1611; the first holder being Sir Anthony who had been knighted by Elizabeth I. Bramshill was bought by Lord Brocket in 1935 and when he left eighteen years later the property was bought by the Home Office and since 1953 it has been used as a Police Staff College.

The Mistletoe Bough Chest

Lieutenant-Colonel the Hon. E. Gerald French, DSO, wrote about Bramshill in 1964 and he told of having lunch there with the thirteenth baronet, Sir Anthony Cope, 'many years ago' and on that occasion first hearing the story of the old oak chest, immortalised by Haynes Bailey in 1828 in the poem 'The Mistletoe Bough' with its haunting stanza —

The mistletoe hung in the castle hall,
The holly branch shone on the old oak wall;
And the Baron's retainers were blithe and gay,
And keeping their Christmas holy day.
The Baron beheld with a father's pride,
His beautiful child, young Lovell's bride . . .

During the course of his article, published in Hampshire: the County Magazine, Lieut-Col. French explores the story that has become known as the legend of the Mistletoe Bough and the possible location. It is a fascinating exercise. In general he feels that certain aspects of the accepted story 'conflict with the theory of invention'. In the version of the story related to Lieut- Col. French, the grief-stricken family, after searching for days without success for their newly-married daughter, leave the house and do not return to it for some two years. The housekeeper, being informed that the family are returning, sets about preparing the beds and in looking for sheets and blankets accompanied by a housemaid, explores a wing that has not been occupied for years and coming upon a chest in one of the rooms, thinks that it might contain some linen and discovers the unfortunate bride's hiding place. The housekeeper's actual words are recorded as 'Oh, they may be in that chest, and yet I do not think it likely. . . ' So distressed are the family when they return home to be met by the sad news that their daughter's body has been found that the entire wing, some forty rooms, is immediately demolished.

Examining the details of the story with great care Lieut-Col. French refers to a book by Sir William Cope (which I examined at Bramshill) where attention is drawn to the amount of detail in the account that came into his possession and the question is asked: 'Could the words of the housekeeper have been invented, for instance?' To add to the intriguing mystery there was an old oak chest at Bramshill for many years, until it was taken away by the widow of the tenth baronet, Sir Denzil Cope, in 1812.

In another book about Bramshill, written by Lady Grant when she was Penelope Cope and only twelve years of age, it is stated that her grandfather, Sir William Cope, wrote to the person who had the chest, claiming it as the property of the family and adding, 'If your heart is in the right place, you will send me back my chest.' A witty reply came back: 'My heart is in the right place — it is in my chest.'

The researches of Lieut-Col. French led him to the conclusion that if a tragedy such as that related in the traditional story did occur at Bramshill and if the victim was a member of the Cope Family (the account quoted by Sir William Cope described the unfortunate girl as 'Miss Cope') then the event must have taken place between the year 1700 when the Copes first occupied Bramshill and 1812 when the chest was removed. During this period only one daughter of the house was married at Bramshill.

In February 1727 Anne, elder daughter of the sixth baronet, Sir John Cope, married Hugh Bethell from Yorkshire. According to Sir William Cope she died in January 1728 or 1729. It seems to have been a common practice in those days to record the date of burial rather than the date of death and since Sir William was obviously uncertain of the year, it is likely that he was equally uncertain whether the date referred to death or burial.

If it is assumed that Anne Cope (Bethell) was buried in January 1729 that would be approximately two years after her marriage and it may be thought that it is within the bounds of possibility that the legend is based on fact and that it all happened at Bramshill. Even the demolition of a wing of the house, to blot out the scene of the tragedy, is consistent with extensive alterations undertaken at this time and described by Sir William Cope in his book.

On the other hand would it be likely that at a wedding in February the bride would carry a sprig of mistletoe — unless of course mistletoe had some significance for the bride or the couple which has become lost over the years. Perhaps the only really puzzling and incomprehensible feature remaining is that in a search extending over several days — even weeks perhaps — those unused rooms would not have been thoroughly searched and yet perhaps it is not beyond possibility that the chest could not have been opened. It is a mystery that, like all good mysteries, deepens as one seeks to fathom it. Perhaps the story of the mistletoe bough is no more than a legend without foundation in fact (but what a grim story...) or perhaps, like most legends, it has its origins in fact. We are never likely to know for sure although there is no questioning the evidence of many responsible people, including the Queen of Romania and her children, when the Rumanian royal family were at Bramshill during the Second World War, that the unexplained figure of a young woman in a white dress and carrying a sprig of mistletoe was seen from time to time. Indeed the Queen requested that her children be given another bedroom on account of the ghostly 'white lady' who they had seen several times in their room at night.

Today at Bramshill an enormous Italian chest stands in the entrance hall, facing the main entrance to this lovely house of mystery. There are no question marks, no doubt in somebody's mind: it is proudly captioned 'The Mistletoe Bough Chest'.

The indisputable Italian origin of the chest now at Bramshill is strange and interesting in itself. Six years before Bailey's work was published a poem had been written with an almost identical theme. The author was Samuel Rogers, a poet and friend of Lord Byron, but the setting was not England but Italy. In the middle of the seventeenth century Sir John Cope, the fifth baronet, travelled widely throughout Europe and among other furniture he brought back from Italy was a marriage chest; possibly, just possibly, the very chest that had figured in the original story. Certainly Rogers believed the story to be founded on fact. Oddly enough the story was current in England at the time that Rogers wrote his poem so the explanation cannot be simply one of transplanting the story to England; perhaps Rogers Italianised an existing English story... it all becomes very confused.

In any case there are other ghosts at Bramshill — even today. Ghosts that may or may not be connected with the carved marriage chest. It has long been said that at midnight in the Long Gallery an aroma of perfume can be detected and on certain nights the figure of a beautiful young woman, dressed in a flowing white gown, runs along the lonely corridors and is sometimes seen walking in the garden.

When I visited Bramshill in August 1980 in the company of my grandson Toby, we were treated to some of the tales of strange happenings that have been reported over the years and to a tour of the historic house by several of the resident staff. Even the police here have had arresting experiences, it would seem!

One of the first Commandants, a distinguished senior soldier, told my friend Dorothea St Hill

Bourne in 1970 that one day he and a police officer saw a figure standing on a little bridge which carries the long drive from the Tudor gatehouse over a stream. The whole length of the mile-long drive was in view from the terrace where the two men were standing. The officer set off to warn the intruder that he was trespassing but it was a puzzled and disgruntled policeman who returned, for when he had reached the bridge no one was in sight, nor was there any nearby cover where someone could have hidden. It was just one of many strange things that have happened in the park surrounding Bramshill. For years horses shied when passing a stretch of water known as the Pale Pond, the haunt of the mysterious Grey Lady, one of the Cope family ghosts.

It is a ghost that was often seen when the Copes lived at Bramshill. Little Penelope Cope was still in her pushchair when her nurse and her mother were not infrequently puzzled when the little girl began to talk about a 'green man' whom she said she often saw about the house and park, generally near water: the lake, a pond, a large puddle or even the child's bath. Asked to describe anything unusual or disturbing about the figure, the child would reply, 'Like Daddy — but no legs.'

Penelope's mother, Mrs Denzil Cope, had been assured on her marriage that she could discount the Bramshill ghost stories but now she was not so sure... especially when she discovered that an eccentric Cope ancestor had a passion for the colour green. He used to dress entirely in green, down to the smallest detail, even carrying a green whip and wearing green gloves; he had his house and furniture painted green and he lived on green fruit and vegetables Only his boots were black for he always wore the fashionable Hessians, unobtainable in green. Could this account for the child seeing no legs?

This strange little man threw himself into the sea and to his death from the cliffs near Brighton in 1806 and one wonders whether the watery manner of his death accounts for his ghost's predilection for water.

The Bramshill Grey Lady has been seen by many people. Mrs Denzil Cope opened her eyes one morning to see a beautiful woman with lovely golden hair and wearing a grey dress leaning over her bed, and the whole room was filled with the aroma of lilies. The same figure, always accompanied by the scent of lilies, appeared several times to the Denzil Cope children in their respective bedrooms and often seemed to pass through solid wooden doors, usually about three o'clock in the morning. The descriptions of the figure supplied by the children were identical to the figure seen by their mother, although they added that there seemed to be a soft light surrounding the ghostly figure whereas the rest of the room was in darkness.

The face of the Grey Lady looked sad and sometimes there appeared to be teardrops on her cheeks while her dark eyes had 'a kind of dead light' in them. Sometimes her hair would be dishevelled as though she had just risen from her bed, untidy ringlets brushing her shoulders and sometimes she would point towards a window. The grey dress she wore was a very plain, straight, sleeveless robe, almost like a shroud.

Another ancestral ghost (or was it the same one, or perhaps the bride of the mistletoe chest) made a dramatic appearance one evening in front of Penelope's great-grandfather, Sir William Cope, and members of his family. The household were on the terrace when suddenly they all saw the white-robed figure of a woman leaning over the balustrade at the far end of the terrace. Thinking that one of the housemaids must be sleepwalking in her nightdress, Sir William sent for the butler to deal with the situation. At first the man could see no one but as he advanced down the terrace, he saw the white-robed figure of a woman leap over the balustrade and disappear. No explanation was ever found for this incident.

Most of the rooms and passages and winding stairways that Toby and I traversed at Bramshill seem to be haunted. There is the ghost of a little old man with a long beard who has been seen peering in at a hall window; there is the Fleur-de-lys room (so called from its decoration) where strange experiences and odd happenings have been reported, one of several bedrooms that have long been reputed to be badly haunted; there is a room on the first floor where ghostly figures have been seen over the years, especially by children; there is the Chapel Drawing Room that some people have seen crowded with people from another age; and the adjoining room, once a bedroom, where the ghost of a woman in the dress of the time of Charles I has been seen, the tight green bodice and full flowered skirt instantly recognised by several witnesses; and there are several rooms which dogs refuse to enter. Once a man in body armour, crossed by a brilliant red sash, was seen in the Chapel Drawing Room and on another occasion, the figure of a woman dressed in the days of Queen Anne.

Yet another room upstairs has a somewhat poignant ghost; a visitor entering the empty room felt the tiny hand of a child pushed into hers and it remained there for several minutes while the visitor had an overwhelming feeling of sadness, as long as the phantom hand held hers. Another room on the first floor is occasionally peopled with apparitions and here, those who see the figures invariably remark that the ghostly forms seem to be floating about two feet above the existing floor. In fact the flooring here had once been that much higher and it would seem that the ghosts are appearing exactly as they appeared before the structural alterations, which make no difference to them. . . indeed they walk right through the walls and doors at Bramshill as elsewhere.

On the same floor, amid the prosaic surroundings of the Police College accounts department, a ghostly aroma resembling lilac has been experienced several times by members of the present staff; but then civilian staff at the college, police wives, a Red Cross worker and two builders are just a few who claim to have seen ghosts at Bramshill.

One employee at Bramshill who had no doubt about the ghosts or at any rate about one ghost was Fred Cook who spent nearly forty years looking after the brooding mansion for the Ministry of Works. With some reluctance he related some of his experiences in 1962. 'I never used to believe in ghosts and when, from time to time, someone would tell me they had seen the Grey Lady, I used to tell them it must have been a trick of the moonlight. It was hard enough to keep maids at Bramshill without people walking about saying they had seen ghosts... Then a footman came down one morning and said a lovely young lady in a grey costume had walked through his bedroom in the middle of the night. I told him there were no such things as ghosts but I don't think the footman believed that. A few mornings later he came down and said the Grey Lady had again walked through his bedroom the previous night and when he saw her he had jumped out of bed and tried to put his arms around her. As he did so she dissolved in his arms and left a strong flowery scent behind her.'

Many people told Mr Cook that they had noticed that certain rooms seemed to be mysteriously filled with the scent of flowers when they entered them and he found that these were always the same rooms although the people who reported the matter to him were unaware of previous reports relating to these rooms.

Then there was the experience of the King and Queen of Romania and their family, of whom Fred Cook was very fond. When Toby and I were at Bramshill we were shown the apparently comfortable room once occupied by the two royal children. Both the King and the Queen had asked Mr Cook to let the children occupy another room because they were disturbed, night after night, by a young lady who walked through the room while they were in bed.

No sooner had the children been given another room than the Queen asked Mr Cook the name of the beautiful young lady staying at Bramshill. 'There isn't one,' replied Fred Cook. But the Queen insisted that there was. 'She was sitting in the King's chair, facing the television. When I looked again she had gone. I neither heard nor saw her come or go'. The description of the ghost seen by the Queen was that of the Grey Lady. On another occasion the Queen saw a young lady in a white dress running along a corridor — presumably the doomed bride.

Then Fred Cook saw the Grey Lady himself. He had made a tour of the house one night at dusk, accompanied by his dog, a big Labrador. 'I opened the door of the Long Gallery,' he said in 1962, 'And there, staring at me, was the Grey Lady. If I was mistaken my dog wasn't. She gave a howl of terror and fell over backwards... then she ran for my home, she couldn't get there fast enough... and I wasn't far behind her...'

After a few minutes Fred Cook remembered his responsibilities and went back to the Long Gallery, leaving his dog, shivering with terror, in front of the fire at his home. He opened the big door quietly and peered cautiously into the haunted, historic, atmosphere-laden Long Gallery. It was completely empty but there lingered everywhere in the enormous room the unmistakable smell of lilies.

As he made his way out of Bramshill and down the drive towards his home, Fred Cook had the distinct impression that something was following him and getting nearer and nearer, something that left him at the gate but something that so frightened him that for the rest of his life he made sure that he never went along that part of the drive alone except in full daylight. As soon as he tried to describe the terrifying feeling to the lady who at that time owned the house he was occupying, she looked at him with an odd expression. 'You are not the only one to have felt the feeling of terror,' she said. 'Every evening I used to take my dogs for a walk. At the exact spot you describe one night I felt completely overcome by a mortal fear. I remember it was dusk on a lovely summer day but I felt a sense of panic and my dogs, who would have stood by me against anything that was made of flesh and blood, had gone racing away ahead of me. I found them cringed with fear, howling, and I shall never go along that walk again if I can help it...'

Not without cause has Bramshill been described as the most haunted house in Hampshire.

BRAMSHOTT NEAR LIPHOOK

Bramshott Church

The green lanes and pleasant corners of this delightful village are reputed to be haunted, indeed, according to Jack Hallam, Bramshott is the most haunted village in England.

The old manor, nestling among the fields at the end of a short lane, has long had the reputation of harbouring a ghostly White Lady who is thought to be Lady Hole, a former owner. There are also, it seems, two male ghosts: a priest from Elizabethan days and someone who looks like a Quaker. I was shown over this really lovely old house when it was empty a few years ago and I can well understand anyone who has lived there wanting to return. There is a still, quiet atmosphere conducive to ghosts and I have no doubt that in its long history there have been owners and occupants who have left behind something of their personality that certain people can still sense.

Another Elizabethan spectre is that of a gamekeeper named Adams whose ghost has been seen sitting outside his cottage enjoying a clay pipe filled with tobacco, which must have been a new-found pleasure in those days. Along the same lane ghostly pipe music has been heard that is said to originate from a fair-haired shepherd boy: since only the music is heard I am not sure how it is known that the music is played by a shepherd boy or that he is fair-haired! But perhaps at one time he was seen as well as heard and now the visual part of the phenomenon has run down, almost like a battery, and only the sound remains.

In the lush and quiet meadow beside the slow-flowing stream there is another ghost that has become known as Mistress Elizabeth Butler. She is said to have been so unhappy that she drowned herself in 1745 and her ghost walks beside the water. Close to the nearby church with its yew trees and thirteenth-century chancel, its beautiful seventeenth-century silver church plate, pewter flagon and portrait medallions; there is yet another ghostly girl. It is said that a little girl in a poke bonnet is seen walking through the churchyard wall and disappearing. One wonders about the story behind such an appearance.

There is also at Bramshott a Grey Lady who lingers beside a well where she is thought to have plunged to her death long, long ago and the village also apparently boasts the ghost of a potboy who still hurries hither and thither with pints of ale as he did in the days when coaches stopped and called for ale to refresh the passengers.

One of the leafy lanes is reputed to be haunted by a host of ghosts in Tudor costume and I remember once asking the horror actor Boris Karloff, who had a house at Bramshott, whether he had ever seen or heard any of the ghosts. He said, 'No, but from my experience of human beings, when they see me in the flesh, the ghosts would probably be so scared that they would disappear before I did!' Karloff's own original and lovely cottage is, I have been told, haunted on occasions by a tall, dark figure and there have been stories of strange and inexplicable noises at night.

The ghosts of Bramshott are, says Jack Hallam, completed with the wraith of a woman with some children who is seen near a lodge house; a phantom coach-and-horses that is reputed to clatter through the village from time to time; a mounted cavalier who rides through a hedge; a murdered highwayman whose faithful horse carries the body of its master through the years; a white calflike creature about the size of a large cat; a black pig that surprises people by suddenly grunting and then disappearing; and another victim of a watery death, though whether by accident or design we do not know. I have to say that I take most of these ghosts with a grain of salt but it is possible to find the odd villager who knows something about one or two of them...

BREAMORE NEAR FORDINGBRIDGE

Breamore House, an Elizabethan manor built in 1583 had been occupied continuously by the family of Sir Westrow Hulse, ninth baronet, for two hundred and twenty years, until he and Lady Hulse moved out in 1968 because of the 'iniquitous taxation of capital and income' and because it was ludicrous to live in a stately home showplace which was 'twenty times too big' for them. They moved into a four-bedroomed thatched Tudor cottage on the estate. The house has long had a 'tradition of haunting' as the Daily Telegraph delicately put it, and I asked Sir Westrow whether he could let me have some information on the matter.

'There has been a regular and persistent story about a ghost at Breamore House which is supposed to appear on the impending death of the current owner,' Sir Westrow told me. 'Maybe that is why I have never seen her!'

The ghost is a lady in a poke bonnet and she is supposed to be Lady Dodington who was murdered in the house by her second son Henry in 1639. He was hanged for the murder at Winchester in 1640. It is said that if the portrait of Lady Dodington is moved from its accustomed place in the Great Hall, her ghost will walk; and there have been instances of visitors to Breamore House, one of the most historic properties in Wessex and open to the public for nearly thirty years, remarking on a sensation of extreme coldness in the Blue Bedroom where the murder took place.

Breamore House

BURITON NEAR PETERSFIELD

Buriton Manor

The Manor House here, where Edward Gibbon (1737 — 94) the historian wrote much of his monumental Decline and Fall of the Roman Empire, is or was at one time so haunted that in 1957 the then owner, Lieut-Col. Algernon Bonham Carter succeeded in getting his rates reduced by £13.00 a year, because his house was haunted!

Mr and Mrs Miller-Sterling, who moved into the house after the death of Lieut-Col. Bonham Carter, told Diana Norman, 'There is no doubt that the Colonel was very psychic and that the house was extremely haunted during his time.'

There is a tradition that a female servant, a

chambermaid, committed suicide in the huge tithe barn facing the house many years ago and it is said that her ghost has been seen and heard going out of the house, across the lawn to the barn, as she must have done before she hanged herself. Where the figure has been seen to vanish into a wall there was once a gateway through the wall.

An underground passage used to lead from the manor to the nearby church and both the late Colonel and his butler said they often heard footsteps walking along the passage towards the church, but they were never heard returning.

Perhaps beautiful Buriton Manor is no longer haunted and yet... in 1962 the Miller-Sterling's five-year-old-son complained several times that 'someone or something' kept trying to remove his pillow at night when he was in bed. Tom Corbett, my clairvoyant friend, told me that when he visited Buriton he distinctly saw the ghost. He said it was an elderly and warm-natured woman who may have been a nanny or children's nurse. He felt the ghost was a friendly one and that she was perhaps trying to make the boy's pillow more comfortable rather than trying to remove it. He said the ghost walked out of the boy's room, down a passage and into another room, perhaps the servant's own bedroom during her lifetime. It may be that the young Miller-Sterling reminded her of one of her young charges long ago.

Children seem to be especially favoured by the

sight of this elderly, smiling woman who watches them at play and there have been several instances of children, some of whom have no previous knowledge of the ghost, suddenly becoming aware that they are being watched and glimpse, just for a moment, the figure of a kindly, homely-looking woman watching them. A maid or nursemaid from the time of Gibbon would seem to answer the general description of this ghost.

There is also, it would seem, a ghost friar at Buriton. Some years ago the son of the occupants was bringing his pony into the stable yard one afternoon when he was surprised to see a man standing beside a bale of straw. The figure was dressed in a long brown cloak and appeared to be a real person; yet, although there was nothing really frightening about the figure, the boy sensed a sensation of menace that seemed to emanate from the silent, solitary, still figure. However the boy said nothing to his parents but something told him to enter a note in his diary as to what he had seen.

A couple of days later his mother noticed the entry and mentioned the matter to the local rector who said he would have a word with the boy who readily described in some detail the figure he had seen. From his description it would appear to have been a friar rather than a monk.

When the story of the boy's experience became known, other people came forward with their stories. A churchwarden revealed that a few months earlier she and her daughter had been picking some wild roses near the Manor when they had seen a man walking towards them; he wore a brown cloak tied with a white cord that ended with tassels. When the figure was almost upon them, it suddenly vanished.

Part of the rectory garden is known as the Monks' Walk and a previous incumbent left records of a brown-robed figure that he had encountered walking along the avenue of beech trees behind the house; a figure that vanished when he started to walk towards it. The canon's wife reported that she had several times heard footsteps that she was unable to account for, from the same area—the Monks' Walk.

BURSLEDON NEAR SOUTHAMPTON

More than thirty years ago Mr Harry Price, Chairman of the Ghost Club, psychical researcher and author of some of the best books about ghosts and haunted houses, told my friend Air Commodore R.C. Jonas that an old house called 'Greyladyes', a rambling place with many odd holes and corners and strangely substantial walls in the cellar, had long been regarded as haunted by the occupants and by local people.

Ghostly forms were reported to have been seen from time to time and an amount of poltergeist-like activity certainly took place there at one time; a particular and peculiar manifestation being the dancing of cups in saucers. One wonders about the origin of the name of the house and whether ghostly grey ladies still haunt the vicinity of the house that was called 'Greyladyes'.

CHILLERTON, SOUTH OF NEWPORT, ISLE OF WIGHT

Back in 1960, when I welcomed him to the Ghost Club, Sir Shane Leslie told me all about the terrifying apparition he saw at haunted Billingham Manor when he lived there. It was, quite simply, the severed head of Charles I. Later, when I visited haunted Brede Place in Sussex, I learned that the first Lady Leslie also saw this frightening phenomenon at the charming two- hundred-and-fifty-year-old manor house.

When Sir Shane and Lady Leslie rented the house in 1928 they knew the well-known story of Charles I escaping from captivity in Carisbrooke Castle and reaching Billingham Manor where he is said to have concealed himself in a very narrow hiding-place, a secret apartment constructed behind a sliding panel in the drawing room. It is said that so uncomfortable was this confinement that the King chose to return to his dungeon at Carisbrooke of his own accord, rather than suffer the agony of the confined space at Billingham, in the hope that a ship would take him to France. Whatever the truth of the story the Leslies discovered a secret space, no bigger than a coffin, which could have been the secret aperture described in the traditional story. What is more their nights were disturbed by the sound of heavy feet and the clank of swords on the stairs and one of the maids saw a man walk through the wall of a room...

One night, or rather very early one morning, when the sounds were so violent that they had awakened the whole household, Sir Shane and Lady Leslie got up to investigate. They all went in a body with the rest of the occupants of the house to the drawing room where the noises seemed to be centred and there they saw a faint light oozing through the cracks around the sliding panel that hid the secret hiding place. When they slid back the panel the brilliance of the phosphorescent light from within the aperture stung their eyes for a moment but when the smarting had ceased everyone in the room saw the same thing. The severed head of Charles I stared out at them from the recess!

Sir Shane Leslie told me that there was no mistaking the apparition: there were the soft ringlets, the pointed beard and the pitiful expression on the face and in the open eyes... gradually, as they watched, too horrified and surprised to make a movement, the spectre faded, the glow subsided and they found themselves looking at an empty aperture as they had seen it so many times before.

During the course of his researches into the history of Billingham House, Sir Shane Leslie came across the diary of a former owner, wherein was described exactly the same arresting phenomenon that he and his household had seen and, said the diarist, he had discovered that on both occasions that the head had been seen, an execution had taken place on the Island. Imagine Sir Shane's astonishment when he discovered that on the day that the severed head had been seen again at Billingham in 1928, a prisoner had been executed at Newport. Sir Shane told me that he believed the King, only too well aware of the distress suffered by the doomed prisoners, was drawn back into the twilight world between reality and oblivion on such occasions.

In 1933 J.B. Priestley was living at Billingham and although he always said he saw nothing to disturb him during his stay at the house, where he wrote some of his books, I have noticed that he never said that he heard nothing and indeed there is good evidence that ghostly noises were heard during the 1930s, and some people saw things they could not explain. His own son, on one occasion, remarked on the little woman who kept looking at him, although his father could see no one; and a relative who came to stay complained of a frightening figure that she encountered on the magnificent Inigo Jones staircase, and then there was the experience of a hard-headed publisher who visited the famous author at Billingham. He too saw a 'smiling woman' several times, whom he took to be the housekeeper, only to learn when he was about to leave the house that there was no housekeeper and in fact at the time there was no woman in the house.

who married a Miss Leigh from nearby Shorwell; but Miss Leigh was in love with a young French nobleman whom she continued to meet secretly after her marriage and, inevitably, one day Worsley came upon his wife and the Frenchman together. He challenged the man to a duel and, in the walled garden, it is said, the duellists met in deadly conflict and the Frenchman was mortally wounded. For some years afterwards Worsley forbade his unhappy wife to leave the house. And Alasdair believed that the ghostly lady in a grey cloak is the sad Mrs Worsley and that the scent of the Madonna lilies, her favourite flowers, accompanies and sometimes replaces appearances of her ghost.

The present owners of Billingham, Mr and Mrs Spencer Forbes, have encountered this mysterious perfume; they have heard the sound of galloping horses; figures of a man and a woman in seventeenth century costume have been seen in the house; clocks have been interfered with; the sound of sweet music has filled the house — and so the haunting of Billingham does not yet seem to have quite run its course.

CHILWORTH NEAR SOUTHAMPTON

Charming, centuries-old Walnut Cottage in Old Chilworth Village has been owned and occupied by the same family for generations. Mrs MacRae's grandfather told her the house had stood empty for a considerable time long ago because of ghostly happenings. Once her grandparents had heard 'something' walk up the stairs behind them one night, enter their bedroom and apparently wash his or her or its hands in the wash basin! In 1942 Mrs MacRae heard exactly the same thing.

A little earlier, in 1940, both Mr and Mrs MacRae were walking home one dark night and when they were about a hundred yards from the cottage, they both saw a great glow spreading over the roof and the chimney stack. They thought the cottage was on fire... but when they reached the house the glow disappeared and they could find nothing to account for what they had seen.

In 1964 Mrs MacRae told my friend Dennis Bardens, the first editor of BBC's Panorama programme, that they occasionally heard a loud knocking on the front door of the cottage but there was never anyone there when they opened the door.

Once a very heavy letterbox rattled as though something had come through but there was nothing to account for the noise. The spring on the letterbox was so heavy that the strongest wind never made it rattle. Once Mrs MacRae and her mother heard the distinct sounds of a horse trotting up to the house but there was no sign of a horse outside. Loud crashing noises have been heard, as though a lot of china had smashed to the ground but again nothing has ever been found to account for the noises.

Time after time footsteps have been heard walking up and down the stairs at dead of night but whenever anyone got up to see what was happening the noises ceased and nothing could be found to explain the noises. Mrs MacRae remembers when she was a girl hearing the same noises and sometimes her father or her brother would get up and search the house, upstairs and downstairs, thinking that someone must have broken in.

On occasions, Mrs MacRae told the *Southern Evening Echo* in 1972, she would be busy doing some housework when something would seem to fall down behind her with a 'swish', almost like a metal bar falling. This had happened at least a dozen times but she never found anything that could have caused the sensation and the noise. Sometimes the dog barked suddenly when there had been no sound that she had heard and there was no sign of anyone being in the vicinity. Could he sense something that she could not see or hear, she wondered.

One night in 1939 Mr MacRae was sleeping alone at Walnut Cottage and he found himself awake in the middle of the night and he became aware of the sound of people talking, and he seemed to see two old men wearing cloth caps with tassels sitting at a table, talking...

One summer night Mrs MacRae found herself suddenly wide awake and she heard the sound of men walking up and down the path and talking in low voices; when they appeared to reach the cottage she decided that they must be some travellers who were lost and she hurriedly got up and opened the door. There was no one there and no footsteps walked away from the cottage.

When her mother was young, she and three sisters had all heard sounds like a big dog or a bear bumping its way up the stairs. It seemed to come into the bedroom and they were all very frightened but they saw nothing and the noise was not repeated. It should be noted that all four girls heard the noise independently.

Today Mrs MacRae and her sister-in-law share this delightful timbered cottage and still ghostly noises are heard. The sound of whispering on the landing upstairs is quite a common occurrence and sometimes the ladies lie awake in the small hours, listening but never quite catching the words. And there are still unexplained footsteps.

'All quite ordinary noises, my dear,' they will tell

you. 'But distinct and for years we both heard them — and other people who stayed here too — before we discussed them and found we were both hearing ordinary noises at unusual times and in unusual circumstances.'

Quite recently, they told me in 1979, they both heard the sounds of someone washing his hands in a room where there are no washing facilities. 'Something unseen once bounded down the stairs,' the ladies related, with awe. 'And one night we heard what sounded like the movement of furniture downstairs when we were in bed, but nothing was moved, it never is...'

CHRISTCHURCH

The Priory Church — once upon a time a priory of Austin Canons — had a chapel that is haunted by a monk. The last Prior of Christchurch was John Draper who died in 1552 and it is the little Draper Chapel, where the mortal remains of the prior rest behind a graceful screen, that is haunted.

We all owe a debt to John Draper for at the Dissolution it was his reputation as an honest man and his friendship with Thomas Cromwell that persuaded Henry VIII to leave the church intact, although the monastic buildings were destroyed. Can it be the ghost of this gentle man that returns occasionally to the place he loved?

A few years ago a young lady, one of a party being taken round the beautiful building enquired from the guide: 'Who was the man dressed like a monk' who had just passed them and gone into the Draper Chapel. In fact another visitor, not attached to the party, was at that moment standing looking at the model of the early priory above the doorway of the Draper Chapel and anyone entering the chapel would have had to pass this visitor who was quite certain that no one had in fact gone into the chapel which was quite deserted. Nor had anyone else seen the robed figure described by the girl who was however obviously sincere in the belief of the reality of what she claimed to have seen. And other visitors have reported seeing a silent, robed monk entering the Draper Chapel.

At one time a spiritualist clairvoyant and medium claimed that he had been in communication with 'John Draper' and with the 'Prior's Cook'. Both had maintained that a great part of the church treasure, mostly gold, had been securely hidden and not handed over to the crown. The treasure was hidden in the grave of one Christopher Stenhouse, said the communicator, but the stone slab of that grave had been reversed and now bore another name. The vicar at the time was interested and reported the matter to the Bishop but there are at least four gravestones in the chancel that have been reversed and used again and as far as I know no action was taken in the matter.

COLDEN COMMON NEAR WINCHESTER

Marwell Hall

My good friend Christina Hole states emphatically in her excellent survey *Haunted England*, 'Jane Seymour's ghost haunted her old home at Marwell Hall'. She continues, 'Perhaps she was revisiting the scenes of her happiest year, for here in May, 1536, she is said to have been secretly married to the King in an upper room. Campion says that her ghost haunted the corridors "where just a year previously she had been preparing for her wedding with Henry VIII while her predecessor, Anne Boleyn awaited execution."'

Jane Seymour, sister of Thomas Seymour of Sudeley, Baron (c.1508 - 49), Lord High Admiral of England and fourth son of Sir John Seymour of Wolf Hall, Wiltshire and younger brother of Edward

Seymour, first Duke of Somerset, certainly became the third wife of Henry VIII in 1536, but whether they were married at Marwell Hall or at Hampton Court seems difficult to establish. Another daughter, Elizabeth, married Thomas Cromwell's son.

When I visited Marwell Hall in August, 1980, with my grandson Toby, the last owner, Mr J.M. Knowles (present Director of Marwell Zoological Park) mentioned that it had been suggested that the marriage between the King and Jane Seymour had in fact taken place before Anne Boleyn had been executed... a traumatic event that might well have prompted the ghostly appearances of Anne Boleyn and Jane Seymour whose ghosts may have been encountered by both Mr Knowles and his wife when they lived at the Hall. Mr Knowles was good enough to talk at some length about historic Marwell and he showed us some of its treasures. On several occasions 'something' was sensed rather than seen in the ground floor corridor on the east side of the house.

Toby and I walked through this 'haunted corridor' when we arrived at this lovely old history-laden house so full of atmosphere, and we strolled along the same corridor as we left to take some photographs but neither of us noticed any psychic atmosphere so perhaps all is quiet and peaceful there now unless we were there at the wrong time... perhaps at night or on a dark wintry day things may be different...

Wendy Boase, in her authoritative *Folklore of*

Hampshire and the Isle of Wight, states that the King married Jane Seymour 'while Anne Boleyn awaited execution... A year later Jane herself was dead and for long haunted the corridors of the old house.'

There is a sadness about Marwell Hall, rebuilt and spoiled in many ways in 1851, but then it is sad when such a lovely place is used mainly as offices. We were shown the enormous carved Seymour fireplace in the library and the ancient Royal Arms in the hall that may once have stood nobly over the front entrance, and the handsome stairway and the beautiful lawns and the graceful arbour where, it is reputed, Henry VIII first placed his hand on Jane Seymour's knee. Marwell was net a place of great happiness and good fortune for the Seymour family and in fact it did not remain long in their possession.

There is a story that following a murder in nearby Owlesbury church, when the then owner of Marwell Hall murdered a priest, the priest cursed the owner and the Hall and said that it would never be inherited beyond the second generation and that it would bring happiness to no man. Whatever the truth of that story it is possible to find grounds for believing that something of the curse has left its mark.

Originally the property belonged to the Bishops of Winchester and it was given by the King to Sir Henry Seymour, a violent-tempered man of strong protestant opinions, but then the Seymours were a violent and determined family. Sir Thomas Seymour intrigued against his brother Edward and sought to procure for himself the position of guardian of the young King, Edward VI; he tried to marry Elizabeth before she came to the throne and when this project was frustrated he secretly married the late king's widow, Catherine Parr. On the death of his wife he renewed efforts to marry the Princess Elizabeth but he was again unsuccessful and eventually he was convicted of treason and executed in 1549.

Events that took place at Marwell may well have triggered off more than one haunting. The ghostly White Lady, long reputed to haunt the Yew Tree Walk, the avenue of yew trees on the north-west side of Marwell Hall, was thought to be Anne Boleyn bringing vengeance on the house of her supplanter, for each appearance of the ghost seemed to be followed by misfortune. Christina Hole feels that this ghost may not be Anne Boleyn at all but some unidentified ancestral ghost connected with Marwell. Reports of the White Lady in the avenue of yews were numerous some years ago and Mrs H.M. Butler, whose father was an employee on the estate in 1930, well remembers her grandmother often relating the story of the White Lady on the Yew Walk. Mrs Butler has always been intrigued by another story concerning the same avenue of trees. At that time the Yew Walk at the back of the Hall went through a field and towards a green door that led on to Owlesbury Road. There was a persistent legend that said that if ever the green door was blocked up the surrounding brickwork would fall into ruin; today the door is blocked and the wall on each side is in ruins. Can there be any connection between the mysterious White Lady, the curious green door, the Yew Walk and the ruined wall?

When Mr Knowles moved into Marwell Hall he was curious about the stories of a White Lady on the Yew Tree Walk, then very prevalent, and on several occasions, he told us, be took a tiger and walked along the avenue that now forms part of the zoological park. Mr Knowles never saw or sensed anything unusual and nor, apparently, did the tiger. Many domestic animals — horses, dogs and cats, are reputed to be psychic and to be immediately aware of any apparition or psychic presence but I don't know about tigers! It was an unusual experiment and one that I have yet to try!

Another version of the cursing of Marwell says that when Henry VIII gave the property to the Seymour family the local priest regarded the matter as church property that had been stolen and he is said to have cursed the entire Seymour family with bell, book and candle and all the powers at his command, saying they would soon lose both house and estate. Tradition has it that when Sir Henry heard this, he had the unfortunate priest dragged from the altar while he was saying Mass and killed on the spot. Yet perhaps the curse was partly effective for Sir Henry's three grandsons were the last Seymours to own Marwell.

Marwell Hall is one of several beautiful houses in Hampshire associated with the Mistletoe Bough story of the body in the carved chest but I think Bramshill has the best claim to that story and so this colourful legend is to be found under the entry for Bramshill — and yet one wonders for notwithstanding that at least five houses in Hampshire claim the story, F.E. Stevens in his *Hampshire Ways* says, concerning the Mistletoe Bough story: 'Marwell Hall, near Owlesbury, was the actual place and there the oak chest stood for many years.'

Firsthand and reliable accounts of strange experiences at Marwell seem to be few and far between these days and perhaps by now whatever haunting there was at that lovely house has run its course but still occasionally one comes across something interesting. A few years ago Mrs N. Clogstown of North Warnsborough related her experiences when she had been a guest at Marwell. In her bedroom at dead of night she heard sounds like heavy footsteps and it seemed as though something big and heavy was rolled and bumped down the stairs. Next day she was shown a hiding-place behind a secret door where, it was said, smugglers used to secrete barrels of contraband. Some strange echoes from the past perhaps still intrude into the present at Marwell Hall...

CRONDALL

The haunted lime avenue leading to Crondall Church

Even the solemn and staid *Victoria History of Hampshire* by William Page, FSA, (1911) mentions that Itchel Manor 'is supposed to be a haunted house; unaccountable noises are said to be heard, but only when members of the family or their dependants are living there.'

Crondall, lying between two other historic and haunted places, Basing House and Farnham Castle, was the scene of several skirmishes between the opposing Royalist and Roundhead garrisons during the Civil War. In 1643 Crondall church was occupied by part of Sir William Waller's army from Farnham, who fortified the churchyard. Records still preserved in the church recall payments for 'making clear the church' and 'beating down earthworks' following these fortifications and perhaps it is not surprising that there are persistent reports that a ghostly Roundhead soldier haunts the churchyard and also that on some moonlit nights a mounted trooper, in Cromwellian uniform, is seen to emerge from a drive opposite the church, ride through a wall and up the avenue of lime trees, vanishing into the church through the closed door. One of these seventeenth century ghosts is said to have disturbed a wedding in recent years.

The now-vanished Itchel Manor House, built in the fifteenth century, burnt down in 1680, rebuilt in 1701 and finally demolished in 1954, was the home of the Lefroy family for a hundred and fifty years and during most of that time various manifestations were constantly being reported by the family, their servants and guests.

There was the phantom coach-and-horses that would be heard driving up to the front door of the manor and stopping. Mrs Arles Edgecombe (nee Lefroy) possessed family papers which revealed that this had happened many times. There is a letter from one guest who heard the distinct and unmistakable sounds while she was changing for a dance. She hurried down to help receive some early guests, as she thought. She waited in the library, but there was no ringing of the front door bell, no one came to answer the door and after a few moments she went out into the entrance hall where she met the butler who told her he, too, thought he had heard the sound of a carriage arriving at the house but in fact no carriage of any kind had come up the drive and there was no sign of anyone on the front porch.

These sounds of a coach and horse arriving at the Manor House were also reported by a new tutor at the house who was sitting up late in the morning room, writing. So frightened did he become by the sounds that apparently had no explanation that he extinguished his light and fled upstairs to his room with the intention of retiring but to his dismay he could not find his room and he wandered up and down corridors and along passages and stairways for what seemed to him like hours until he was eventually rescued by his host. Thereafter he insisted on being escorted to his room last thing at night!

On 10 October, 1973, following a talk that I gave on Ghosts at Ewshot, I was introduced by Barbara Cross (author of *The Ewshot Story*, 1973) to a young lady whose grandfather had heard the ghostly carriage wheels that have long been associated with the haunting of Itchel Manor. So distinct and real were these sounds that the man stepped aside to make way and after the sounds passed him, he saw there was nothing visible making the sounds.... His family were inclined to regard the story with scepticism but to the end of his days he always insisted that he had heard those inexplicable sounds, the only experience of a possibly paranormal nature that he had encountered in a long life.

There is a story among the family papers to the

effect that before the Lefroys came to the manor the owner was set upon by a highwayman while driving over Bagshot Heath. The postillion and the man himself were shot dead and the horses bolted for home, galloping up the drive and coming to a stop at the front door of the manor. The owner's wife hurried out to meet her husband, only to find him dead in the carriage. Can this be the origin of the ghost coach-and-horses? Another story concerns 'Squire Bathurst' — the Bathurst family owned the Manor for about a hundred years, from 1670 until the middle of the eighteenth century — and it is said that the squire was stabbed to death in his carriage by an Italian servant. Barbara Cross reveals that unaccountable noises used to be heard in certain rooms of the manor and when the old house was pulled down a portrait of this 'rather formidable old gentleman' was discovered behind the panelling in one of the bedrooms.

In his history of Crondall the Revd C.D. Stooks writes of Itchel Manor as 'a well authenticated instance of a haunted house' but reiterates the tradition that the noises were, usually, heard only by members of the Lefory family and their dependants. Mr Stooks himself spent a night in the haunted room, apparently, but did not hear or see anything of any ghost. Strange noises continued to be reported after the haunted part of the house was rebuilt.

It certainly seems that unaccountable noises

constituted the main haunting at Itchel Manor. Rappings and thumps were heard in many parts of the house and were never explained. At one time the heavy thumps and bangings at dead of night were thought to be restless horses and at length the old stables were pulled down and rebuilt farther away from the house — but still unexplained sounds continued to be heard, as frequent and as loud as ever.

One room at the Manor was known as the Little Highlander and seemed to be particularly haunted. Once a member of the family, Charles Lefroy, was writing there late at night when he heard footsteps coming up the stairs and approaching the door of the room he was occupying. He heard the sounds stop outside the door but when he opened the door, no one was there and there was no sign or sound of any physical person having been there. Then he heard a cry and thinking that one of his children was awake and frightened he went to the nursery but found all the children quiet and sleeping soundly. Next morning the nurse confirmed that all the children had slept quietly all night but she too had heard footsteps before Charles Lefroy had visited the nursery.

One wintry night an occupant of Itchel Manor heard the sound of a flock of sheep immediately outside his window. He wrestled with his conscience as to whether he should go and drive them away but decided it was too cold and he turned over and went to sleep to the sound of the bleating sheep.

Next morning there were no signs of any sheep having been anywhere near the house and no sign of any damage.

One evening old Mrs Elizabeth Lefroy was reading family prayers when she stopped for a moment in the middle of a sentence and then continued. At the end of the devotions she forbade anyone to leave the room until she returned. She searched the house from top to bottom to try to find the origin of the footsteps she had heard, although she knew the house was deserted. No one else was in the house at the time and she was satisfied that the sounds she had heard had no normal explanation.

On another occasion when the same Mrs Lefroy was ill she asked who had not been at prayers because she had again heard footsteps outside the room she was occupying. Every member of the household was accounted for but the footsteps continued to be heard from time to time

At one period in the eighteenth century the Manor was, as we have seen, owned by a miserly character who is said to have met a violent end and 'Squire Bathurst' was long reputed to haunt his old home. There are stories of his having been surprised as he gloated over his hoards of money and murdered by one of his servants and then bricked up in the walls of the house. Another version of the story has it that the Squire murdered his valet. The former story seems perhaps the most likely since Squire Bathurst was undoubtedly eccentric and bad-tempered, treating his servants with contempt and even physical cruelty and there is evidence to suggest that there were several motives for the valet murdering the Squire but few for the boot being on the other foot.

Ghostly sounds at Itchel Manor were fully written up by a certain Captain Fraser who visited the house in 1840. Both he and his host, one of the Leforys, to whom the property passed in 1818, heard muffled thuds on the walls around midnight; blows that began slowly and rhythmically and then became irregular, less frequent, and weaker; sounds that might be consistent with the story of the bricked-up Squire trying to attract attention or endeavouring to batter his way out. Captain Fraser heard the noises on three occasions, apparently emanating from different parts of the house and varying to considerable degrees in their intensity. It seems indisputable that these noises were heard intermittently by various people for many years.

During all the years that the Lefroys were at the old manor they had the greatest difficulty in keeping servants who always complained of peculiar noises which started nearly every night about eleven o'clock. At first it was thought that the sounds might originate in the nearby bailiff's house, but this was found not to be so and indeed the noises continued to disturb and trouble the occupants of the old house after the bailiff's house was demolished.

At the time that Captain Fraser wrote up the long account of his experiences Mr Lefroy told him that he had once slept in one of the rooms where the noises sometimes seemed to originate and he had been disturbed by a sound like a heavily-laden cart or carriage passing below the window. He had looked out at once but could see nothing to account for the sounds although it was a clear and moonlit night. Eleven years afterwards his uncle had exactly the same experience while occupying the same room.

If a murder took place at old Itchel Manor no details are available and it is by no means certain that a murder took place at all. There is however a very strong tradition that some sort of violent death occurred in the house in the days of Squire Bathurst and it is difficult to doubt that from this period peculiar noises were heard on many occasions by varied, disinterested and reliable people.

According to an undated extract from a report in a local paper the ghost of a uniformed soldier has been seen in the vicinity of Crondall church in recent years. I am indebted to Dorothea St Hill Bourne for this firsthand account which took place during the 1939-1945 war:

'Last night, Wednesday 2 November, being a very fine moonlit night, a friend suggested that we should enjoy an hour's cycle ride so we set off to Crondall. The time was 10.15 p.m. when we reached the church. We had left our cycles against the wall of the churchyard and were about to go up the lime avenue to the church when we noticed a misty object coming, it seemed to us, from a carriage drive opposite the wall. We stood perfectly still and waited to see what it really was when, to our amazement, we saw it was a rider on horseback, dressed in what looked like the armour of Cromwellian days. Whatever it was rode right through the churchyard wall, up the avenue, and disappeared, it seemed to us, into the church. We waited about half-an-hour, hoping it would return, but we did not see it again.'

The late Mrs Edgecombe of Shalford, Guildford, was present at the wedding of Katherine Lefroy in Crondall Church. Before the wedding there had been rumours of the ghost having been seen in the vicinity of the church and during the service, while the congregation were standing, heavy footsteps were heard clumping from end to end of the church roof, apparently between the ceiling and the roof itself. The bride's mother was so upset that she suddenly sat down and had to be revived with smelling salts. A cousin dashed up the stairs to the room but no one was up there and the shape of the present roof makes it impossible for anyone to walk along it; furthermore, people waiting in the churchyard confirmed that no one had gone up there.

In March 1971 Colonel Cromwell told Dorothea St Hill Bourne that he had interviewed a local man he knew who had also seen the Cromwellian ghost. One Christmas, about thirty years previously, he had been walking home from a dance at Crookham with a friend and after parting from his friend, he was passing Crondall Church when he saw a mounted figure in armour ride through two double doors of a house opposite the church, through the wall, up the avenue of trees to the church and there hammer on the church door: he distinctly heard the reverberating knocks. He was so frightened that he would never go that way again at night, but took the long way round another road.

Erlands House is reputed to have a Regency ghost, the pleasant spectre of a man in a blue Regency coat who has been seen several times by different people leaning against a mantlepiece. Montgomery's Farm is also haunted, according to Dorothea St Hill Bourne, but she has no details.

DODPITS CROSS NEAR NEWBRIDGE, ISLE OF WIGHT

The signpost here may be haunted according to a contribution in the Islander in May, 1973. Mildred Morris recounts an experience she has never forgotten. She was walking home from school one October evening in 1928 and she had almost reached Dodpits Cross. She was in a happy frame of mind and was in fact looking forward to her evening meal. Suddenly she realised that the signpost looked different. It was much taller than she remembered, higher and bigger altogether. And as she slowly walked nearer she saw that it was a gallows and that the body of a man was swinging from it. She was not afraid, merely curious, and she distinctly saw the man's head, held tight in a noose, was bearded and that his long black and curly hair reached down to her shoulders. He wore a dark cloak and while one foot retained a long boot the other foot wore a stocking and the boot lay on the ground. Sightless eyes met those of the curious girl — and suddenly she was afraid and she raced for home...

When she recovered a little and looked back the gibbet and hanged man had completely disappeared and the signpost had re-appeared, just as she had always seen it previously and as she always saw it afterwards. Her mother laughed at her imagination but her grandmother wasn't so sure. She said Dodpits meant 'Pits of the Dead' and her grandmother had told her that in the eighteenth century men were hanged at crossroads... Could that practice or the phantom gibbet be the reason for the bridle path leading to Dodpits Cross being called, since time immemorial, Dark Lane?

EAST WELLOW
NEAR ROMSEY

Florence Nightingale knew this village as a child; she was here when she was at the height of her fame — and it is here that she lies buried. I well remember talking to her friend Sir Harry Verney about the days he would take her for drives along these leafy lanes, for she dearly loved Hampshire. It is nice to know that although the nation would have buried her in Westminster Abbey, she rests in Hampshire soil.

There is a legend that when you open the ancient door of the church of St Margarets, as she must often have done, and your eyes fall on Saint Christopher carrying the child, you are safe for the day. And there are other legends and ghosts at East Wellow. The vicinity of the church is said to be haunted by the ghost of a Cromwellian soldier, one Colonel William Norton, who walks from the chine to the old manor house, where he once lived.

Embley Park, the home of Florence Nightingale, is also reputedly haunted, but not by the saintly lady of the lamp, but by a phantom coach-and-horses, driven by a spectral coachman, that rushes across the fields and meadows from the house, now a school, to the church.

FARNBOROUGH

Farnborough Place

In 1953 there was a considerable stir locally when Farnborough Place, the old Manor House and now Saint Peter's School, was said to be haunted by the ghost of a middle-aged woman.

There are records to show that Edward Dickinson bought Farnborough Place in 1619 and on his death in 1630 the property was sold for the benefit of his sons and daughters. His eldest daughter married Richard Sterne, great-grandfather of Lawrence Sterne, author of Tristram Shandy and A Sentimental Journey. By 1652 Farnborough Place had become one of the seats of the Earls of Anglesey and one of the Annesley family, while in residence at Farnborough Place, figured in a law case which is reconstructed by Sir Walter Scott in Guy Mannering.

The Wilmot family acquired the property in 1768 and they entertained at their home people like Sir Joshua Reynolds (who painted a portrait of two members of the family) and David Garrick, who is remembered by a marble tablet in a wall and some lines which he composed to a favourite cat. 'Pretty, witty' Nell Gwynne is reputed to have been in the habit of staying at the house in the reign of Charles II. Farnborough Place was the residence of the lords of the manor for nearly three hundred years; parts of the building are supposed to date back to the reign of King John and the house is said to have been restored by Sir Christopher Wren. There are also stories of a secret tunnel running from the house to the church. With so much history and so many singular individuals associated with the house, could it not be haunted?

At the time of the 1953 disturbances the property was used as an advanced jet-engine college and senior Service officers and hard-headed engineers were among those who claimed to see the ghost. Mr Donald Brown, principal of the college at the time, said he 'regularly heard the ghost walking about'.

Among members of his staff who said they had actually seen the ghost, wearing a long brown robe and a large hat, was housekeeper Mrs Evelyn Bell who stated: 'The figure moves but makes no effort to speak and quickly vanishes when it is seen. It is not possible to distinguish its features... I last saw it about a fortnight ago', she added in January 1953.

On one occasion a visitor to the college was cycling up the drive when she saw the figure and, thinking it was Mrs Bell, stopped to speak but the figure seemed to walk into a tree and vanish. Some of the students who resided in the old house had equally frightening experiences and so did some of the senior staff.

Commander M.W. Peters, a director of aircraft maintenance and repairs at the Admiralty stated at the time: 'I woke up one night feeling chilled to the bone and with my hair literally standing on end with fear. Yet nobody had told me anything about the house being haunted.'

An Australian engineer decided to investigate for himself when he heard footsteps in a room above him which he thought was unoccupied and empty. As he opened his bedroom door he heard footsteps coming down the deserted stairs and his courage failed him... he leaped back into bed and pulled the sheets over his head!

At one period, due to the effect the apparent haunting was having on many of the students, Mr Brown included in each course a serious lecture on psychic phenomena, pointing out that there was no need to be frightened. But he was a man after my own heart for, in the interests of psychical research, he always postponed giving the lecture until the newly-arrived students and senior staff had slept two nights in the haunted house!

There are many stories of ghosts at Farnborough in the old days. A well-known ghost was that of a headless old woman who used to be seen sitting on a gate in Highgate Lane on winter nights. In her lifetime she had been regarded as a witch by the local people and her ghost was accepted as returning to the places she had known during her lifetime. It is said that on one occasion a waggon and four horses remained for several hours in one place in Highgate Lane because the driver could not get the horses to pass the ghost of the old woman.

Writer Nancy Spain flew from Farnborough airfield on the flight that ended in her death and there have been reports that her ghost has been seen there on the anniversary of her death.

FLEET

There is a long-standing tradition that Bagwell Lane in haunted and has been haunted for many years by a mysterious White Lady. Some people associate the ghost with the suicide of a woman in a nearby pond about a century ago.

Certainly there have been many instances of people of varying ages encountering a figure dressed in white or a very light-coloured dress, suddenly appearing before them and as suddenly and mysteriously disappearing. A few years ago three witnesses stated that they saw a white figure glide across the road, over a field, and disappear in the vicinity of a pond. Although the White Lady seemed to enter the deep pond, the surface of the water did not appear to be disturbed.

In May 1968 a motorcyclist reported that the figure of a young woman suddenly seemed to glide in front of him, dressed in a white gown or dress. He quickly braked and when he had stopped and recovered from the surprise of her abrupt appearance, he turned round and saw the same white figure standing in the middle of the road. He had had enough of the White Lady of Bagwell Lane and he set his face for home and did not turn round again!

Another person who encountered this occasional phantom told me that she usually seemed to be seen by young people and when he saw her he noticed, in the split second that he did see her, that her face appeared to be sad and wet but it was a young face with the hair dressed in an old-fashioned manner. One moment the road was totally deserted, the next moment he was almost on top of the white form as he cycled along, and the next moment she had completely disappeared.

FOUR MARKS

On the Winchester Road, just down the hill from Four Marks, there is an inn called the Watercress Inn. It used to be called Nip's Inn and before that The Shant, but whatever name it goes by the ghost stays put.

This rather isolated public house was built about a hundred years ago to accommodate workmen who were building the railway line; many of these came from Dorset and 'shant', I am told, is a Dorset term for a measure of beer.

The original inn was built in front of a three-hundred-year-old cottage which has since been converted into a restaurant but in uncovering some of the old oak beams which had been plastered over for so long, the builders brought back memories of an unusual and unsolved mystery.

One night in 1912 the landlady of the inn was busy serving drinks to a crowd of customers in the bar when suddenly, for some unspecified reason, she went through a door and into a back room — and she was never seen again. One local historian has it that there was a wild party at The Shant that night with regulars and visitors drawing their own beer and not being too careful about payment!

At all events the structural alterations seem to have disturbed the psychic atmosphere at the old inn and in 1978 the landlord, Nip Sandell and his wife saw the ghost of the mysterious former landlady. They have heard no odd sounds but they have caught more than a glimpse, on more than one occasion, of a gliding female form or shape. So far they have not discovered any possible solution to the mystery of her sudden disappearance but perhaps one day...

FRESHWATER, ISLE OF WIGHT

It is impossible to think of Freshwater without thinking of Alfred, Lord Tennyson, who really loved this place and there is a granite column on the summit of High Down to commemorate the walks he used to make in all weathers to revel in the glorious views. His old home at Farringford is now a hotel but there are those who say they have seen the quiet shade of Tennyson, a familiar figure in his day with green topcoat and big- brimmed hat, taking again the walks he so enjoyed before he became so famous that he was pestered by tourists and eventually left the Island and died at Blackdown near Haslemere. It is only right that if his ghost does walk, it does so in the vicinity of his beloved Freshwater.

Golden Hill Fort, built to defend the Island against invasion by Napoleon, has appropriately enough, the ghost of an unidentified sailor. The figure, seemingly solid and lifelike, has been seen late at night, standing in a doorway, with his arms folded, relaxed and resting as so many sailors must have stood in that spot in the long history of the hexagonal building.

The local story to account for the appearance of the ghost sailor says that he was hanged by his mates for treason, inside the fort, at the top of a flight of steps. No story is extant, as far as I have been able to discover, pertaining to the ghost of another sailor, or possibly a soldier, dating, from his dress, from the First World War.

Witnesses to other strange happenings at Golden Hill Fort have included a girl who used to work there. One evening she heard footsteps although she thought she was alone in the place. As she hurriedly prepared to leave, she heard the footsteps apparently enter the room she was occupying! By this time she was so anxious to leave the Fort that she tripped and fell and cut her head... by the time she had picked herself up all was quiet, much to her relief.

FROYLE

An old village that seems to lack all recorded history and is unusual in having many cottages with niches containing representatives of holy figures. A former rector, the Revd L. A. Pickett, tells me that the statues were placed where they are by Sir Hubert Miller who was the squire who owned the houses and most of the land in Froyle. He was a great churchman and had a tremendous devotion to the saints. He acquired the statues during his many journeys abroad. His own patron saint is over the little Post Office and Saint Paul is in a niche at the Vicarage.

The old vicarage was thought to be haunted at one time. I have records from Mrs Sangster who believed that there was a ghost there when her husband was vicar. Some of the Sangsters' visitors heard and felt things they were totally unable to explain. One priest utterly refused to stay in the house after one night as he said it was 'too busy'. Two friends of mine, without knowing anything of the experiences of other people, felt very uncomfortable in an upstairs room that was used as a drawing-room and also in one bedroom that contained a very old four-poster bed.

Later they learned from Mrs Sangster that her

husband's predecessor used to see the ghost of an old man sitting in the upstairs drawing room, since pulled down. A psychic lady visited the Sangsters and said the room was very haunted and a priest who came to stay with them left on the Sunday evening (although booked to play golf with Mr Sangster next day) because he said he couldn't stand the incessant whispering in his bedroom at night.

Froyle Vicarage

HARTLEY MAUDITT

In the volume of *Hampshire* in his famous King's England Series, Arthur Mee opens his brief mention of Hartley Mauditt with the words: 'Its wide pond keeps lonely company with its church. . .' And well it might for this is a haunted area.

The quaint little church contains some interesting mediaeval paving, mostly depicting foliage and eagles but two bear enigmatic fish designs, unique in the country. Dating from about 1150 the church contains the original Norman chancel, two Norman windows and a series of memorials to the Stuart family whose Manor House once stood next to the church but has 'mysteriously' disappeared.

The house was traditionally defended against a troop of Roundheads by a certain Nicholas Stuart and perhaps it was destroyed at that time, but at the Restoration, Nicholas Stuart seems to have received back his lands and become the first Baronet of Hartley Mauditt. After several generations the family sold the property to the Stawells.

Henry, the last Lord Stawell, whom we have already met at Marelands, Bentley, was by all accounts an unpleasant, unprepossessing and evil-looking man, certainly in his later years. Ralph Dutton tells me that he once owned a portrait (it was lost in a fire) that showed a round, fleshy face with small, cunning-looking eyes, sparse hair and practically no neck. He married, when he was twenty-two and she was nineteen, Mary Curzon, daughter of Viscount Curzon of Penn and, again to quote Ralph Dutton, 'one has the impression that they were both difficult people'. There are stories that she preferred the manor of Hartley Mauditt and was determined to live there, whereupon the 'wicked' Lord Stawell peevishly demolished the property, almost over her head.

Parts of the old Manor can be seen, I believe, in other houses in the country. Part of the staircase has been incorporated into municipal offices, some floor tiles are to be found in a nearby rectory, and one of the original entrance lodges functions as a cottage. But nothing remains of old Hartley Mauditt Manor itself except perhaps for an underground passage to Selborne Priory, linking the few remains of the Manor cellars which, standing in a dark group of trees, have long been reputed to be haunted by a 'white lady': the unhappy Lady Stawell, no doubt.

Furthermore they say that a ghostly coach- and-four sometimes rattles down what was once the drive to the Manor, skirting the silent pool and the little church from which ghostly music has been heard to emanate.

HEADLEY

A few years ago my wife and I visited a detached house here, that was at the time the home of an army commander, his wife and four children; three beautiful girls who where then aged twenty-three, twenty and seventeen and a son who was mostly away at university. The two older girls were also at university so that the usual residents comprised the Commander (who told me that he had experienced nothing of the reputed haunting), his wife and Harriet, the youngest daughter.

The spacious and well-appointed house had a plain but impressive exterior and a circular front drive; it stood well off the road, shielded by a tall hedge and trees and behind the house there were some six-and-a-half acres of rough pasture. The house was built about 1935 and was first occupied by a naval commander and his wife. After the commander died his widow sold the house to an army man and his wife and they used to let the property and eventually sold it to the present owner. As far as is known neither family who previously owned the house was troubled by any psychic activity.

There is no documentary evidence of a former property occupying the site but the land is extremely old and the many species of trees and shrubs on the property are evidence of the many years during which this stretch of land has hardly changed. There are traces of a pond at the far end of the pasture land and slight traces of a cart track in the meadow, a track that presumably ran across land where later owners built a double garage and where much of the reported phenomena occurred. It is likely that the field was used for watering horses and cattle for hundreds of years and this use may have been reflected in the name of the property.

Within a couple of weeks of moving into the house odd things were being noticed and they continued to occur, with increasing frequency, right up to the time I first visited the place, with the latest incident taking place only four or five days previously.

Nine-tenths of the happenings originated outside the house and most of them were sited in the area of the garage forecourt. No precise dates were available to me but the family often felt an oppressive and unwelcoming atmosphere in that part of the property and occasionally inside the house. All the family found it difficult to concentrate and the son (although sceptical of anything pertaining to ghosts) even got into the habit of going to a friend's house whenever he wanted to write letters. Both Harriett and her mother told us that whenever they go away, or even when they go out, they hate returning to the house and always feel that they are unwelcome and almost as though something is trying to urge them out of the house. Most of the incidents seemed to take place at dusk. Apart from the figure of an unidentified man all the disturbances were auditory.

This figure of a working man was seen passing the kitchen window, apparently going in the direction of the garage. It was first seen by the Commander's wife within weeks of moving into the house and she naturally enough thought it must be a real workman of some kind, but knowing that he had no business there she went outside to see what he was up to and outside the house there was no trace of any man. Subsequently the same form was seen by other female members of the family and Harriet told us that the form was glimpsed rather than seen, that there was no time to see the face but that one got the impression of a working man, wearing a jacket, passing the window. Once two men were seen, the usual one and another who wore a cap. As well as the lady of the house and her three daughters, this figure was also seen by a relative who stayed at the house for three months and knew nothing about the previously reported appearances.

The second reported phenomenon was heavy footsteps. These were so loud that they sounded like a horse being backed into shafts rather than footsteps made by a human being and the sounds came from the concreted area in front of the garage yet they sounded as though they were on gravel. On occasions these noises, originating in the open at night, although nothing was visible, kept people in the house awake for hours. The two younger daughters also heard this noise as well as a visiting friend.

Inexplicable groans were heard, loud and distressing, by two of the daughters and by their mother, while they were inside the house but the noise seemed to come from outside, again in the vicinity of the concreted forecourt. The noises were distinctly localized but nothing could be found to account for them. Another distressing noise was the sound of a baby crying, which just went on and on, fading and returning; extremely worrying and upsetting for the hearers. We were told that it was difficult to describe the exact quality of this sound but it seemed to the hearers to be removed in some strange way, almost like an echo.

Other apparently equally inexplicable sounds were described to us as grunts, sighs, clicks and a particularly common and unnerving one: the sound of something soft, like a cat, being thrown against the outside wall of the house, sometimes followed by a scratching sound. Once when Harriet heard this noise she heard, too, a faint scream. These noises, when they were heard, seemed to permeate the whole house but always they seemed to come from outside. The domestic pets of the family, a short-coated dog and a cat, seemed to be completely unaffected by the incidents, we were told.

Another terrifying and worrying noise was heard by the two younger daughters and by their mother. This was described to us as a very loud rushing noise, 'like tin wings in a vortex'; it seemed to fill the air and the whole atmosphere appeared to vibrate. Eventually the noise seemed to lift and rise and go away leaving a feeling of space, an emptiness or void, in the air. Once the middle daughter, Clare, heard the noise when she was halfway down the meadow, near an old oak tree. At first she merely thought that it was an odd sound and wondered what it could be but as it grew louder and louder until it seemed to fill the air around her, she became very frightened and ran indoors. Her sister Harriet was the only other person in the house at the time and she told us that Clare was extremely distressed; she flew to her room, exhausted and almost overcome by the experience and indeed she had to resort to a sedative and had obviously had a most unpleasant experience. This particular noise had been heard perhaps half-a-dozen times in all.

Another odd occurrence was the 'appearance' of 'cold spots' in various parts of the house from time to time. These, again, were experienced by the mother and her daughters but they had not noticed any correlation between the discovery of a cold spot and subsequent phenomena; indeed they had not noticed any pattern of predictability, or cyclic element in the disturbances which seemed to happen completely at random, although invariably around twilight or dusk and all the witnesses agreed that at the time of our first visit the incidents were increasing rather than decreasing.

There had also been two unexplained fires; both outside the house. First a deep-litter had caught fire (quite inexplicably, we were told) and later a shed was found alight in the vicinity of the haunted spot in front of the garage.

Always the Commander's wife and her daughters, and her son too, felt that the whole atmosphere of the house and its immediate vicinity was hostile and mentally exhausting; sometimes they felt that they could stand it no longer and in fact the house was at one time put on the market. It does seem indisputable that one of the reasons for the family thinking of leaving was the overall unpleasant atmosphere and 'feel' of the place together with the strange things that had been seen and heard by most of the family. Once a friend of Harriet's, not a practising medium but a sensitive who was much interested in haunted houses and atmosphere, stopped suddenly as he was passing the house and said he felt that something really awful had happened there.

One odd incident did occur inside the house. Harriet was upstairs carrying a tray with crockery on it one evening when it seemed to be drawn out of her hands. She told us it was taken completely from her and dropped gently to the floor where it came quietly to rest without anything breaking or even being upset.

It was suggested that it might be interesting to hold a seance at the house and we did later visit the house with a medium but the results were inconclusive and unsatisfactory; although we were all startled when a cupboard door suddenly threw itself open...

In studying the reported incidents I noticed that most of them seemed to have been experienced by one witness at a time although on occasions a second incident had followed within half-an-hour. The Commander's wife had experienced most of the reported happenings initially but at least one incident was first reported by one of the daughters.

All the family struck us as good witnesses, open to the possibility of a normal explanation for some of the noises and aware of the way in which one's mind can become tuned to accept an 'atmosphere' once it has been suggested; ready and willing to freely discuss their experiences and anxious for any help or explanation.

It seems possible that there has been a tragedy of some kind there or on the site and perhaps the presence of four youngsters nine years previously had provided the requisite environment necessary for some kind of psychic reproduction which continued, perhaps fed by the psychic awareness, by unhappiness, by frustration or by concentrated thought by one or more of the occupants.

From the incidents described it is possible to

postulate some sort of tragedy that might account for most of the disturbances. Perhaps a baby had been murdered by being thrown or smashed against the wall of a property that may have formerly occupied the site of the present house (the sound of a baby crying, fading and returning; the sound of something soft thudding against the wall); a man (perhaps the murderer) takes the body past where the kitchen window now looks out and disposes of it, perhaps down a well or by burying it, in the place now occupied by the concrete forecourt of the garage. It may be the groans of the child's mother as she witnesses the murder or waits for the murderer to complete his task; other sounds may originate from a horse being put back into the shafts of a carriage or cart (carrying the infant's mother) from which the horse has been removed for watering; an excuse possibly to come to the area and do the evil deed there. The grunts and sighs and other noises may be associated with the original work in digging and burying the little body and in the event of some such theory having had any reality, the single scream, the 'hostile' atmosphere and many other incidents could easily fit in. The deed was evidently committed at twilight or evening and the cold spots, the fires and the rushing wind in a vortex may be some psychic way of extracting energy to produce other phenomena. But perhaps this takes us from the realm of reality through that of conjecture into the world of fantasy. The alternative was that it is all in the minds of the witnesses and that, to my mind, seems unlikely.

HERRIARD, BETWEEN ALTON AND BASINGSTOKE

A sleepy village with lovely tree-lined lanes, an avenue of fine beeches, a church with ancient coloured glass and a mystery.

Just off Bagmore Lane and only a few hundred yards from a cluster of cottages, a mound without a headstone marks a grave, but who lies there is one mystery. Another is who tends the grave for it has been lovingly tended for the best part of two hundred years! Somebody must visit the lonely grave and keep it tidy and place fresh flowers there but who and why is a question that the villagers have been asking themselves for as long as anyone can remember.

It seems that the parents of the oldest villagers and their grandparents before them were just as puzzled and there was talk from time to time of strangers visiting the grave and tending it in the middle of the night. Over the years more than one all-night vigil has been kept but the mystery has not been solved for nobody has ever been seen cutting the grass and placing fresh flowers on the grave.

William Annette, who has lived all his seventy-five years in the village said, in 1980: 'Ever since I was a boy I can remember flowers appearing mysteriously on the grave. People used to call it the "Gipsy grave" and one story tells of a gipsy who hanged herself and was buried there.'

Leslie Baptist, once the village policeman, knows all there is to be known about the grave. The story he heard was that a gipsy was killed when his wagon overturned at the spot and he was subsequently buried there. At one time, when he was in the police force, he made up his mind that he would find the answer to the mystery and he used to visit the camps of any visiting Romanies and he became friendly with the gipsy people. He spent hours sitting round their fires listening to their stories but whenever he mentioned the grave, they always became silent and he never solved the mystery.

John Loveys Jervoise, who lives up at the Queen Anne manor house, always understood the grave to be that of a gipsy who was hanged for stealing sheep; that was what his mother had told him. . . . So who lies beneath the turf that is tended by unseen hands: a suicide, the victim of an accident, or a thief? All the local stories say the person buried there is a gipsy but more than that remains uncertain.

During the summer of 1980 the grass on the grave grew long and the villagers of Harriard began to think that at last the mysterious visitors had ended their visits to tend the grave but one day at the end of August the news spread quickly through the village; the grass had been cut and cleared away from the gipsy grave, fresh flowers were on the grassy mound and, something that had not happened before, a crude cross made of hazel twigs lay on the grave — hazel the magical tree with power against all enchantments and evil spirits, hazel the protective...

The immediate vicinity of the grave has a haunted reputation, perhaps understandably; and people say they have felt suddenly cold as they passed the grave and have had the impression of being watched as they hurried on their way in the twilight of an autumn evening. Ex-policeman Leslie Baptist said in 1980: 'I have cycled past the grave many times. The place has a creepy aura about it. Pedalling up the slight rise towards the grave, I used to get a cold, clammy feeling. As soon as I was past the grave the feeling completely disappeared.'

HINTON AMPNER
NEAR ALRESFORD

Hinton Ampner

The Tudor Manor House, demolished in 1793, was the scene of remarkable and unexplained happenings for some twenty years. The house is thought to have been built early in the sixteenth century, replacing a mediaeval building destroyed by fire.

Sir Thomas Stewkeley lived here at the end of that century and as a country seat, the sprawling E-shaped manor was later occupied by his descendants. One of them, Mary Stewkeley, married Edward Stawell (later Lord Stawell) in 1719. Her younger sister, Honoria, lived with them and when Mary died in 1740 an affair developed between Lord Stawell and his sister-in-law who had continued to live at the Manor after the death of her sister. There were stories of 'wild happenings' and a baby is supposed to have been born and to have been murdered. Honoria died in 1754 and there is a plaque to her memory in nearby Hinton Ampner church.

Lord Stawell died in 1755 and very soon afterwards a groom at the Manor declared that one bright moonlit night he had seen the ghost of the fourth Baron, his former master, 'in drab-coloured clothing'. Apart from servants, the furnished house was unoccupied for some years except during the shooting seasons. In January, 1765, the property was let to the Ricketts Family.

Mrs Mary Ricketts is the chief witness in this case and it is worthwhile noting that she came from a distinguished family, her brother having been created Baron Jervis of Meaford and Earl Saint Vincent for his naval exploits. Like George Washington, Mary Ricketts was regarded as being unable to tell a lie. In 1757 she had married William Henry Ricketts of Jamaica and when his business took him to the West Indies, which was quite frequently, she stayed at home with their three children.

When the Ricketts moved into the Manor they took with them an entirely new set of servants from London, complete strangers to Hinton Ampner and its tales of ghosts; but almost immediately the family and servants were disturbed by the continual noise of slamming doors for which no normal explanation was ever discovered. New locks were fitted to all the doors in the house but the unexplained slamming noises continued and six months after the Ricketts moved in, Elizabeth Brelsford, nurse to eight- month-old Henry Ricketts, plainly saw 'a gentleman in a drab-coloured suit of clothes' go into the yellow bedchamber, which was the apartment usually occupied by the lady of the house. The groom, George Turner, maintained that he saw the same 'gentleman in drab clothes' one night. This would seem to be the identical figure seen in the house ten years earlier.

Later the form of a dark woman dressed in dark clothes which rustled like silk was seen and heard one evening by four servants who were in the kitchen. Noises described as 'dismal groans' and 'rustling' were reported soon afterwards, most frequently in the vicinity of bedsteads. A couple of years later, during one of William Ricketts' trips to Jamaica, his wife and all three children frequently heard the noise of footsteps and the rustling of silk clothes against the bedroom door; sometimes the sounds were loud enough to awaken Mrs. Ricketts. In spite of persistent searches, no physical explanation was ever found for these noises. A couple of months later Mrs Ricketts again heard footsteps, heavy and distinct; and about the same period she reported hearing the sound of music and heavy knocks which had no physical reality. About a year later a curious murmuring sound was often heard throughout the house, like a wind beginning to rise;

and a maid stated that she heard a great deal of groaning and fluttering in her bedroom.

Early in 1770 an old man living at West Meon called at the Manor and asked to see Mrs Ricketts. He explained that his wife had often told him that in her young days a carpenter whom she knew well had related how he had once been sent for by Sir Hugh Stewkeley and on his direction had taken up some boards in the dining room to enable Sir Hugh to conceal something beneath them. Afterwards the boards were replaced.

In the summer of 1770 Mrs Ricketts, lying in bed in the yellow bedchamber, 'thoroughly awake' as she put it, for she had retired only a short while before, plainly heard the plodding footsteps of a man approaching the foot of her bed. She felt the danger to be too near for her to ring the bell for assistance so she sprang out of bed and fled to the adjoining nursery, returning with a light and the children's nurse. A thorough search revealed no trace of an intruder or any cause for the noise she had heard. There was only one door to the bedroom, the one leading into the nursery. For some months after this experience Mrs Ricketts was undisturbed in the yellow bedchamber until, having moved to a warmer room over the hall, she sometimes heard in the November 'the sounds of harmony' and, one night, three distinct knocks. A little later she often noticed a kind of hollow murmuring 'that seemed to possess the whole house', a noise that was heard on the calmest nights.

On 2 April, 1771, the sixteenth anniversary of Lord Stawell's death, a number of unexplained noises were heard at the house by Mrs Ricketts and some of the servants, including three heavy and distinct knocks. A month later the disturbance increased and by midsummer they had reached a hitherto unparalleled level. The sounds of a woman and two men talking were a frequent phenomenon at this time. These sounds were heard night after night. Usually a shrill female voice first, followed by two deeper men's voices. Although the conversation sounded close at hand, no words could be distinguished. Loud crashing noises and piercing shrieks followed which died away as though sinking into the earth and a nurse, Hannah Streeter, who expressed a wish to hear more, was thereafter troubled every night!

Mrs Ricketts' brother, the future Lord St Vincent, arranged to sit up with Captain Luttrell, a friend, and a servant. Night after night they heard loud noises, as of a gun being let off nearby, followed by groans; there were rustlings, door- slamming, footsteps and other sounds which convinced Captain Jervis and Captain Luttrell that the house was unfit as a residence for any human being.

Early in August 1771, Captain Jervis left the house and his sister and her children followed soon afterwards. The Bishop of Winchester allowed Mrs Ricketts to live at the Old Palace — the Manor of

Hinton Ampner originally belonged to the Priory of Saint Swithin at Winchester and was the particular perquisite of the Almoner, whose title became attached to the place and gradually became corrupted to Ampner. Later the Bishop of St Asaph offered Mrs Ricketts his house in London, where she lived before renting a house in Curzon Street.

There can be no doubt that the experiences at Hinton Ampner Manor House so terrified Mrs Ricketts that she had to leave the place and in particular one curious experience of which she gives no details, merely saying: 'I was assailed by a noise I never heard before, very near me, and the terror I felt cannot be described.'

Towards the end of the Ricketts tenancy of the house a reward of £50, then £60 and finally £100 (a lot of money in those days) was offered for the solution of the disturbances; the money was never claimed.

A year after Mrs Ricketts and her family left Hinton Ampner, the Manor was let to a family named Lawrence who endeavoured, by threats to the servants, to stifle reports of disturbances. Little information about the curious happenings undoubtedly experienced at this time leaked out although it does seem that the apparition of a woman was seen. The Lawrences, who were the last inhabitants of the property, left suddenly in 1773 and the house stood empty, apart from its ghosts, for over twenty years, when it was demolished.

The Hinton Ampner case is exceptionally well documented in the form of contemporary letters from Mrs Ricketts to her husband in Jamaica and to the Revd J.M. Newbolt, Rector of Hinton Ampner. There are also letters from Mrs Ricketts' brother to William Ricketts, and various letters from servants to Mrs Ricketts; but perhaps the most moving evidence is contained in an account, written in 1772, which Mrs Rocketts left for her children and for posterity. I have consulted all the original documents concerned with this fascinating case and reproduce in full Mrs Ricketts' account in my volume Hauntings (J.M. Dent 1977) where I also reproduce for the first time the recollections of the ghost story compiled by Lady Mary Long in 1862.

The fourth Baron Stawell's daughter, who was created Baroness Stawell, married the Rt. Hon. Henry Bilson-Legge and their granddaughter, an only surviving child, married in 1803 John Dutton, second Baron Sherborne. The present owner, Ralph Stawell Dutton, FSA, is their great-grandson.

A new Hinton Ampner House was built about 1793 some fifty yards from the site of the old building and this Georgian house forms the central part of the present building. During the demolition of the old manor a small skull was discovered under the floorboards in one of the rooms.

The present owner tells me that there were some reports of unexplained noises being heard in the new house, usually just before dawn, but between 1936 and 1939 the house was much altered and in 1960 the main part was gutted by fire. Mr Dutton says there have been no apparently paranormal happenings in the present delightful house.

HOLYBOURNE NEAR ALTON

A charming little village left in peace by the building of a busy bypass, Holybourne acquired its name from the pond which has been rescued and preserved, largely by the hard work of local residents. Long years ago men and women trudging wearily along the Pilgrims' Way would stop at Holybourne and wash in the waters of the pool with its reputed healing properties, especially beneficial, it was said, to those with failing sight. Today it is a beautiful and peaceful oasis amid a hive of activity nearby.

Holybourne has a cottage named by a ghost. When the present occupant bought the rose-covered cottage some years ago she was told that there was a friendly ghost, a Grey Lady long associated with the house. Soon after she moved in she had a vivid dream, or vision, or hallucination, or visitation in which the ghostly Grey Lady manifested and intimated that her name was Anne and she would be so happy if the cottage, which had once been named after her, could revert to 'Anne's Cottage'. So it was re-named and today the ghost is a happy and peaceful presence who is still seen occasionally by the occupant frequenting her old home which she, the Grey Lady, evidently loved as much as the present owner.

Just across the A31 from Holybourne is Neatham with its historic Neatham Grange where once stood the oratory founded by Eleanor, sister of Henry III and wife of Simon de Montfort.

There is a gracious house here, still called Neatham Grange, with a Georgian front but much, much earlier cellars and foundations where, if we are to believe the occasional witness, the gentle shades of the unhappy Eleanor and the deeply religious Simon still return occasionally to the site of the oratory provided by their generosity.

The present occupants tell me that they heard the sound of footsteps, many times, from upstairs when their two daughters were younger. Always both children were asleep when their parents investigated. The footsteps have not been heard for some years now. Mrs Wilkinson mentioned this puzzling phenomenon to a gardener they then had and he told her that many years ago he was courting one of the maids and on several occasions they both heard footsteps from the upper part of the house when nobody was there. He also said that a dog lying at the foot of the stairs showed every sign of being terrified by the sounds, all its hackles rising. The gardener never mentioned this before as he was not supposed to be inside the house with his girlfriend.

There have long been stories of an underground passage between Neatham Grange and the now defunct monastery at Monkwood and one old man, now dead, swore that many years ago a local farmer lost two ploughing horses and the plough when the passage roof collapsed, but I have been unable to trace any confirmation of this story.

The monks built the now-vanished oratory and the original grange and their possessions included an ancient water-mill and here too, on still summer nights, the quiet, misty forms of Eleanor and Simon return occasionally to the place they loved in life. It is even said that the wheel of Neatham Mill sometimes turns by itself at dead of night, Dorothea St Hill Bourne was told when she was there in 1966, and water splashes through the millrace of its own accord... Do the monks return to the scene of their loving toil, invisible but leaving tangible evidence of their presence? Can the love and affection that Eleanor and Simon had for Neatham, bridge seven centuries and can their forms still be seen by those who have the eyes to see, or are those silent shades the stuff that dreams are made of?

KIMPTON NEAR ANDOVER

The Kimpton Down Inn, on the edge of Salisbury Plain, became the centre of a considerable amount of poltergeist-like activity, according to numerous well-attested accounts, when structural alterations took place about fifteen years ago.

Reported happenings included ornaments jumping off shelves, plates turning themselves upside down (sometimes when the plates contained food) and bottles, empty and full, being lifted from shelves and racks and dropped to the floor where they smashed.

At one time the daughter of the licensee saw something that was described as 'the faint outline of a figure' one afternoon and subsequently the same indistinct form was seen by the girl's mother and by several customers — who had no previous knowledge of the sighting by the mother and daughter. The form seems only to have been seen during the afternoon and early evening.

Things became so bad at one time that one of the brewery delivery men refused to make deliveries to the public house because he was frightened by the strange happenings. The area manager for Strongs and a surveyor who visited the Kimpton Down

Inn admitted that they felt unaccountably uneasy while exploring the premises.

Locally the disturbances were put down to the death of a former landlord's wife who is said to have died in the cellar. For some reason she is reputed to have been locked in and left to die. The reported activity might be thought to be such as an annoyed wife might resort to — but, as far as I know, there was no expert investigation that might have yielded further interesting information.

KNIGHTON, ISLE OF WIGHT

Knighton Gorges, from an old engraving

The Knighton Estate, where once stood the magnificently gloomy and atmospheric Knighton Manor or Knighton Gorges, perched on its bluff on the river edge, was — and perhaps still is — haunted by the Knighton horseman: a tall figure in medieval costume, elegant in cape billowing behind him as he gallops his black steed over the quiet fields and lonely meadows and, when he reaches the lanes and roadways, the pounding hooves echo in the silent, moonlit night... So the story goes and it is said that there are people living today who remember the sudden chill of fear as the sounds of those approaching hooves steal into the quiet of the night and ring loud and louder still as the phantom horse and rider pass by — some say the rider is headless...

The frightening apparition was reportedly heard and seen by young and old, men and women, who, wide-eyed, stole a glimpse into the moonlit countryside when the sounds were at their height; but most of the country folk preferred to remain shut tight in their homes on moonlit nights for odd stories circulated about strange happenings in the vicinity of Knighton House after darkness had fallen. There is a legend that says a wizard once cursed a knight, at Knighton Gorges Manor House and after his death the ghost of the knight, mounted on a black horse, galloped down to the manor. Night after night the figure was seen and if, over the years, the sightings have become less frequent, still, if we are to believe some of the local people, the Black Knight still rides.

The Norman/Elizabethan manor house, one of the finest mansions on the Island, brooded over the valley for centuries; its massive walls at the same time protective and resistant, oppressive and impenetrable; its colourful history grim with whispers of cruelty and terror. An early feudal owner, Hugh de Morville, one of Henry II's knights, was one of the four murderers of Thomas a Becket and afterwards they sheltered at Carisbrooke Castle. A later owner, Sir Ralph de Gorges, became a Crusader and died in the Holy Land. It was while the house was in the possession of the de Gorges, for more than a century, from around 1241, that the house became known as Knighton Gorges, a name that has been synonymous with mystery, intrigue and ghosts ever since.

After possession successively by the Hacket and Gilbert families, in 1563 the property passed to the Dillingtons of Dorset and finally, in the early years of the nineteenth century, to Maurice George Bissett, on whose instructions the house was eventually and completely demolished. But it seems likely that all these owners of Knighton Gorges and their families and servants contributed in one way and another to the various hauntings associated with this romantic and tragic house.

There is the sweet music that wafts on the evening breeze in the vicinity of the spot where once stood Knighton Gorges; strange, ethereal music that seems to come from nowhere, lasts a few moments and then, almost as soon as the hearer becomes aware of the sound, it disappears. There is the Black Knight that races silently down the incline from the house at Hallowe'en; and there is the hideous, shapeless lump of phantom that used to haunt the house, rattling its chains; now it haunts the site.

During the occupancy of the de Gorges there is a legend that a member of the family sought out one of the ghosts and succeeded in imprisoning it in one of the upper rooms, securing it there for all time by placing a Latin inscription over the door which was sealed and the room was never used again.

Some years later a certain Sir Theobald Russell,

Lord of Yelverland, married into the de Gorges family and was mortally wounded during the French attack on Bembridge and Saint Helens; bleeding profusely he was brought to Knighton Gorges where he died in the room that became known as the 'Room of Tears'. Or, as I had it put to me:'Sir Theobald defeated a mass invasion of the island by the French in 1341 and was slain in his hour of victory'. Here, in the 'Room of Tears' the haunting consisted of the sudden sound of sobbing, so heart-rending in its intensity that all who heard it began to sob themselves, whereupon the phantom sobbing would cease.

During the occupancy of each family there have been mysterious and strange stories associated with the house. Human bones have been discovered in places where a body would seem to have been hidden; there are whispers of murder and wicked deeds and ghastly events that have resulted in the occasional wail of agony that is still to be heard at dead of night; there is the spectral hound that creeps, bleeding from the treatment it has received from its cruel masters; and there is the phantom coach-and-horses that has been seen at least half a dozen times in the past fifty years.

In 1712 Sir Tristram Dillington, MP for Newport, inherited Knighton. A dashing figure, an excellent and generous host, a good master — he was popular throughout the area with rich and poor alike. Then, early in the summer of 1721, tragedy struck the merry Guards major. His wife and four children, including his heir, all contracted a fever. Within a fortnight all were dead and lie buried in Newchurch parish churchyard. Sir Tristram never recovered from this blow. Within weeks he had changed into a morose and bitter man and on 4 July, in despair such as few men can have known, he drowned himself in the pond or lake below the house.

His faithful butler, aware of his master's grief, had begun to keep an eye on Sir Tristram and, too late to prevent his master's fatal plunge, he quickly recovered the body — but it was too late to save Sir Tristram's life. The butler was a shrewd man with a deep sense of loyalty to the family and he thought quickly. As the law then stood, all the possessions of a suicide were confiscated by the Crown. Sir Tristram had left two unmarried sisters who would thus become penniless. . . the butler hastily summoned the head gardener and concocted a plan to save the family property. They broke the girth of Sir Tristram's favourite horse, set the animal loose beside the pool and then raised a hue and cry that there had been an accident and Sir Tristram had been thrown into the pool and drowned. The trick worked. The authorities accepted the story and the two sisters inherited the estate — and in due course the butler was given a farm as a reward. A variation of the story says Sir Tristram shot himself and the butler made it look like an accident. Whatever the truth of the matter, Sir Tristram did not rest and soon many of the tenants on the estate were reporting that they had seen his ghost, 'with troubled face and weary tread' walking silently about the terrace of his former home and about the grounds of his estate where once he had been so happy. More and more frequently were reported appearances of the ghost and at length a priest from nearby Brading conducted a service of exorcism.

But still the ghosts walked. The sad shade of Sir Tristram was still seen wandering pathetically about the house where he and his wife and children had once lived happy lives; an unidentified headless horseman still haunted the lanes and bridle-paths of the estate; mournful wails and sobs still emanated from the 'Room of Tears'; cries of anguish and despair still came from the sealed room and gentle and melodious music still wafted on the night air when it was least expected.

Through the female line Knighton Gorges descended to General Maurice Bockland in the middle of the eighteenth century and at his great house on the Island he entertained many famous people of his day: Sir Joshua Reynolds, actor David Garrick, and ugly John Wilkes of ill repute. . . but Bockland's daughter married into an old Scottish family and instead of happier days Knighton Gorges passed in due course to their son, Maurice George Bissett, who has been described as 'an unscrupulous, selfish bigot'. Certainly he caused a scandal by running off with the beautiful wife of Sir Richard Wosley who sued Bissett for £20,000. The sensational case did nobody any good. Captain Bissett became the butt of London society and suffered a savage caricature; Sir Richard was said to have condoned his wife's promiscuity; Lady Wosley must have been highly outraged when copies of the evidence were openly hawked in the streets of London. . . In the end the jury found for Sir Richard; his wife's affections had been alienated and they awarded him one shilling!

Captain Maurice Bissett's troubles were not yet over. He disapproved of his daughter's choice of a husband and forbade her to marry the man of her choosing. Consequently the couple eloped and married anyway. Bissett was furious and he disinherited her and swore that she and her husband would never set foot in Knighton Gorges. The couple ignored the threats, biding their time until the old man died. But he meant what he said and, shortly before his death in 1821, he enlisted the services of an army of workmen and labourers and he ordered them to completely demolish the house that had been described as 'by far the most considerable and beautiful of the ancient mansions on the Island.'

Down came the tall chimneys, the great walls, the mellow tiles, the heavy doors, the fine mullioned windows, the ceilings, the floors, the panelling and the stonework. By the time that Captain Maurice Bissett died, on December 16, 1821, only the great cellars gaped open to the sky and a pair of stone gateposts were all that remained of a magnificent gateway that led to the grand old house. Today only a few crumbling walls, a grass-covered mound, a ruined stable and the solitary stone pillars of the gateway remain to remind us of a former glory.

And still the ghosts are not placated and strange stories linger about this sad region. It is still possible to find local people who believe that in the 1930s a young man, on a winter's walking tour of the Island, knocked at the door of a house in Newchurch and asked about lodging for the night. During supper he told a strange story. He said he had been walking up the long drive to a big house when he had nearly been knocked down by a carriage-and-horses that thundered by him and he had strode on to the house, determined to complain. When he reached the house, ablaze with light and alive with the sound of music and revelry, no one had answered his repeated knocking. At length he had peered though a window into a lighted and crowded room where everyone seemed to be wearing Georgian costumes. Some fancy dress party, he had thought, rapping even more loudly on the door and window, but still no one took any notice and eventually he walked away and reached Newchurch. He tried to point out on the map exactly where the house and drive were but all the map showed was the site of Knighton Gorges, raised to the ground more than a century earlier.

In her book England's Island Garden author Ethel

Hargrove tells of seeing the great house of Knighton Gorges restored to all its splendour, lights in the windows, dogs baying in the courtyard, sound of carriages on the driveway; and Miss Hargrove and a friend saw a man in eighteenth century costume on the terrace. It was a never-to-be-forgotten experience, that New Year's Eve in 1915 — and yet, something very like it happened a few years later.

Ethel Hargrove together with four friends heard a flood of melody rise from the site of the former mansion a little before midnight and the distinct sound of tenor and soprano voices; the music of a harpsichord playing a minuet and the faint sound of a duet. A few minutes later the party seemed to break up, they all heard a pistol shot, a dog barked, the sound of carriage wheels sounded in the place where there had once been a drive — and then silence.

Even the stone pillars seem to be haunted. A correspondent from the Island in 1972 enquired of a newspaper about the 'figures' that had adorned these gateposts 'a few weeks ago'. The following week another correspondent recalled the pillars being surmounted by animals that seemed to be a cross between a lion and a dog. Photographs taken sixty years ago show that the pillars were only topped by stone roundels known locally as 'loaves of bread'. Do these haunted pillars sometimes revert to their former elegance? A local coach driver used to point out the landmarks to visitors and he always thought there were animal figures atop the pillars and some friends he took to see the gateposts said they saw them too, according to Gay Steedman and Roy Anker.

And still there are mysteries to be solved at Knighton. When the house was demolished a bricked-up recess in one of the walls revealed the remains of a human skeleton; more ancient human remains were found when the pool was dragged. Who is the dark knight and who is the headless horseman that are still seen occasionally if we believe the local people and why does the massive structure of the doomed manor at Knighton sometimes reappear on New Year's Eve? Many indeed are the dark secrets of Knighton Gorges.

LANGRISH NEAR PETERSFIELD

Bordean House

Attractive Langrish village has long been full of tales of secret tunnels, hidden passages and concealed hiding places for this village, although now a long way from the sea, was once at the end of one of the smuggling routes from the coast.

Today the place is best known for having within its boundary one of those excellent Sue Ryder Homes. This is Bordean House, a dignified seventeenth century property built by Roger Langrish and a private residence until 1976.

A hundred years ago the house was the property of the Nicholson family and it remained in their possession until the Second World War. A member of that family, Dr Christabel Nicholson, who was in charge of the Charing Cross Hospital during the War, was at one time Hon. Secretary of the Ghost Club and she was a staunch and faithful member all her life. From Christabel I first heard of the ghosts of Bordean House.

There are generally thought to be four ghosts, two separate ones and a pair, and it would seem likely that they date from different periods. The best known is the White Lady who is nearly always seen walking away from the house, down the drive, where she disappears from sight. Christabel told me that she saw this figure several times and once a naval officer was walking towards the house at the time and she saw the two figures pass on the drive. Christabel met her friend when he arrived at the house but in answer to her questions he said he had passed no one on the drive — which is undoubtedly true; if he had passed a ghost he was not saying!

Another time Christabel Nicholson saw the figure leaving the house and she managed to tell her brother who was in the garden at the back of the house at the time. He immediately went by a roundabout route to the gate and was in time to see the figure approach. He said afterwards that he had never felt so frightened in his life but the noiseless figure passed him without seeming to notice him and when he looked round, after it had passed, the figure had completely disappeared. He said the face was that of a woman of about thirty years of age and she looked very strained and as though she had been crying.

Another ghost at Bordean House is that of a Cavalier who has occasionally been glimpsed, over a period of sixty years or so, in various ground floor rooms but most often in one of the passages leading to the hali. He always seems to be in a great hurry and suddenly flashes by but witnesses have noticed his plumed hat, the feathers swaying at the fast pace and his long cloak billowing out behind him. Once or twice, Dr Nicholson told me, visitors to the house, without knowing anything about the reputed ghosts, remarked on the sudden gust of cold air they had encountered in that particular passage and they thought they had heard the clink or rattle of a sword; but perhaps these sounds belong to the third ghostly appearance, a pair of duellists.

These protagonists were, so runs the story, brothers but the cause or reason for their duel is not know. It seems that one of them received a fatal injury and an 'everlasting bloodstain' on the floor of the chapel has long been pointed out as proof of the story. Dr Nicholson always associated the duel with the sad-faced woman in white and she thought either this woman must have been the cause of the fight or that she left the house shocked and saddened at the idea of two brothers fighting over her — or at the result... alas, I fear we shall never know for sure.

LANGSTONE NEAR HAVANT

At the foot of the old toll bridge leading to Hayling Island, in a property that had once been part of a water mill, Fred Bason told me about the only ghost that he had ever encountered.

Fred Bason was a remarkable and delightful man, an author, bookseller, broadcaster and lecturer. He wrote sixteen books including three very well-received Diaries, and he listed his recreations in *Who's Who* as 'meeting people and making them laugh; encouraging writers by lecturing... and he added: 'visitors welcomed any Thursday... Telephone — none, Clubs — none,' He once told me that he was inspired to write by James Agate and helped at the beginning by W. Somerset Maugham, who wrote introductions to his first two books.

It was during the Second World War that Fred Bason went to live in a large loft that belonged to a friend and there he wrote some of his early books. But I will let him tell the story in his own words: 'Langstone was then a lovely village of about twenty houses, a shop and an inn. I've not been there for years but I like to think that it is still unspoilt... Anyway, I had been working for five days on my book when I felt I just had to have a good walk and some fresh air. It was ten o'clock in the morning.

The sun was shining and the birds were singing. I felt fine. There were no clouds in my skies. Suddenly, in a lane that led to the marshes, I stopped. I felt strangely uneasy. I was suddenly very cold. There was an unfamiliar tingling at the top of my spine that I knew was fear. Then I saw it.

'No more than twenty feet ahead of me on the ground lay an old man. He was completely naked and had only half of his right leg. There was around him a sort of mist, but I could see the figure utterly clearly. He had a hawk-like nose and his chest was covered with long matted grey hair. His head was nearly bald. I would put his age at around seventy. He was very thin and I would think that he would be around six feet tall or maybe a little more.

'I walked a couple of paces forward and then stopped. I looked around me. There was an uncanny silence. I walked forward again and I couldn't have been more than twelve feet away from the old man when suddenly he vanished completely. He didn't fade away, he vanished entirely. I was not drunk, at ten past ten in the morning... I do believe my own eyes. I saw the ghost for between ten and twelve seconds, no longer; but it was an unnerving experience. It was not an eidetic image — a memory image — since I'd never seen such a man before.

'I sat on the bank of that leafy lane and got out my notebook and drew a rough picture of the head and chest of the old man, and then added a rough drawing of the rest of that body with the position of the right stump leg. Then I drew a reasonable map of the lane in relation to the village, and put a cross as near as possible to the place where I had seen the ghost. I suppose it took me half-an-hour to do the job to the best of my ability. Then I put away my book and tried to banish the entire incident from my mind.

'I must confess that time and again as the months passed the mystery returned and I was simply dying to tell someone about it, though I was sure no one would believe me. Eventually I made it one of my topics of conversation at dinners, and in talks that I gave at clubs I would give a brief outline of the uncanny affair. Twice I wrote about the Langstone ghost in magazines. I reckon about five years had passed since I saw the one-legged ghost when there called at my home in Walworth a Mr Edward Greer.

'He told me that he had made the journey from Havant just to see me. Then he drew out from the inside pocket of his tweed jacket a sheet of cartridge paper, and on it was drawn in Indian ink the figure of an old man with a hawk-like, Duke of Wellington nose, matted hair on the chest, and one leg. It was a sketch of my ghost.

'I recognised it at once. I asked Mr Greer to sit down. I poured him out a sherry and asked him to wait a minute. It took me some time to find the notebook but eventually I did and brought it back to Mr Greer. I opened it at the page on which I had drawn my sketch of the ghost and put it side by side with Mr Greer's sketch. They were twins in every detail. No one in the world had ever seen my drawing made on the spot years before.

'Mr Greer made the journey to see me to get confirmation of his own experience, because he had seen the same ghost in the same lane some five years before me. He had made enquiries about the old man, and after drawing a blank for months, he had eventually come across somebody who remembered him. The one-legged man had been an evangelist. He was always seen with a large haversack slung over one shoulder which contained miniature Bibles and small New Testaments, pamphlets and tiny coloured texts. Although he always looked very shabby and must often have been hungry, he never asked for money, or sold anything. He would go up to all and sundry and ask them, "Are you saved?" He would give away a text or a Bible, and his one concern was to save people's souls.

'He was last seen alive in Hampshire late in 1932 or early in 1933. Mr Greer saw the figure in 1939, and I am assured that Mrs E. Bird of Oxford saw the same figure in 1940 — yes, in the same lane — not quite the same part, but in pretty nearly the same position on the ground. With Mr Greer I had a witness of the most unimpeachable character. I was on firmer ground, so I wrote again about the ghost, giving much more detail. The Society for Psychical Research and the Ghost Club wrote to me, asking for more details. But I had no more to give. I offered to go to the spot with anyone but they said there was no need. They took our word. And at that point the matter rested...

'Except that in December 1965, on a bleak evening, I saw the exact double of my ghost, with the same hawk-like nose, a battered trilby hat, and a very tattered coat and he carried a haversack. Did that haversack contain Bibles and texts and religious pamphlets? I simply had to know.

'I stood at his side for a moment and then said, "Pardon me, don't think that I am mad or rude, but I am looking at you, and it seems I'm looking at a live ghost." Then I explained as closely as I could all about Langstone and Mr Greer. I wanted to show him the sketch that I'd drawn. He listened. He wouldn't show me the contents of his haversack. He would not tell me how he lost half his leg. He refused to say how he made a living, save "Oh, bits and pieces, fiddling, and a bit of a pension." he said he was called Pat but refused any surname. I offered him the cost of a meal and his fares if he would come home to see my sketch of the ghost; he would then see with his own eyes his exact image.

'He had been leaning against the wall during most of this rather one-sided conversation. He said it had 'pleasured' him to meet me — not an expression that I had heard before. "Perhaps some when we would meet again." He used the word "when" instead of "time". He held out his thin and ugly long-nailed hand. It was cold, cold as death. Shaking hands with him was very unpleasant. He hobbled away and had gone perhaps six hops, when he turned and said, "Well, are you saved?" And then he vanished'.

Well, that's Fred Bason's ghost story. He showed me the sketch and the map, faded with age and obviously much studied over the years. He told me: "The story is absolutely true; it is the only ghost I have ever seen in my life; it happened exactly as I have told it to you. Maybe you can explain it, I can't..." I couldn't, either.

The centuries old Royal Oak Inn at Langstone Village is reputedly haunted by the ghost of a female who appears in one of the bedrooms; a figure that disappears into a wall when it is spoken to; and by the sound of inexplicable footsteps on the stairs and noises like chairs being dragged over a stone floor. Strange sounds have been reported from empty rooms and in 1970 some guests occupying the room next to the haunted chamber, had booked in for a week but stayed only one night.

At one time the dog belonging to the occupants resolutely refused to be left alone in the 'haunted room' and although other witnesses for the haunting entity are somewhat scarce, it does seem indisputable that an unidentified female form in white walks here on rare occasions, possibly someone who was connected with the old bakery that once occupied the site of the present low, white-washed inn that certainly incorporates a much older property still, and squats comfortably on the edge of the tidal creek. One local man told me that he believed the ghost was that of a girl who drowned herself on her wedding night.

LIPHOOK

The Royal Anchor Inn

The Royal Anchor Inn, where I have enjoyed many a good meal, entertained some honoured guests in the days when it was an important posting house on the main coaching road to Portsmouth. The redoubtable Blucher, the Prussian field marshal and Prince of Wahlstadt, stayed there, with other notables. Pepys notes in his diary a visit with his wife in 1668 and Queen Victoria was there as a little girl with her mother, the Duchess of Kent; and later with Albert. Queen Anne stayed there, and King William IV, Lord Nelson, the Duke of Wellington, and King George IV when Prince Regent; Queen Elizabeth I, James I, Charles II... Tradition even has it that Edward II visited the inn in 1310. And, as befits such an historic inn, the Royal Anchor has a ghost but not a royal one, nor even an important or famous personage for it is said the ghost is that of a highwayman, Captain Jacques, who once plied his trade in the area around Liphook.

The story goes that at last the dishonourable Captain was cornered in Room Number 6 by the Excisemen and he was shot down as he tried to hide himself in a secret passageway that had an entrance behind the fireplace. One Australian visitor, occupying Room 6 at the Royal Anchor, and without any knowledge of the previous reputed haunting, came down to breakfast on her first morning and asked the landlord at the time whether there was a ghost at the inn. No less than three times during the night, she said, a man in a long coat and three-cornered hat came, 'out of the fireplace' and walked across the room and through the closed door. . . On the third occasion this intrepid lady said she had opened the door and followed the mysterious figure but 'he' had vanished in the passage at the top of the stairs and she, sensible woman that she was, had returned to her bed and to an undisturbed sleep for the rest of the night.

The lanes around Liphook have reputedly been haunted for centuries by a boy and his flute. The ghost was often seen, it is said, about the turn of the century. A typical account from that time tells of a man riding home through the woods one evening when he heard a beautiful melody coming from the top of a rise in the ground. As he approached a clump of trees the music became louder and he suddenly saw a boy walking beside a horse and playing the gentle tune on a flute. He rode just behind the boy for a short distance and then attempted to draw level with him and to look at the boy more closely for he was astonished at the beautiful music that the boy was producing. Before he could do so a bramble knocked his hat over his eyes, and at the same time the tantalising music stopped abruptly. When the rider lifted his hat from his eyes there was no sign of the boy, his horse or his magical music. The strange gaiety of the music, the association of trees, and the dislike of being looked at too closely have suggested to some authorities that the 'boy' may have belonged to the fairy kingdom rather than to the spirit world.

LISS

The old name was Lyss and old things are important here. The ancient church of Saint Peter's has a Norman tower and traces of the graves of two Crusaders.

Flint arrowheads, spearheads and axes from long ago have been unearthed here and now reside in the British Museum. A curious story tells of the discovery of a hard black lump, like a piece of coal, inside a hollowed-out tree trunk. After it had been inside the home of the person who discovered it for some time, the black fragment unfolded itself and proved to be hair, the hair of some dark lady who lived at Lyss two thousand years ago and must have been buried before the death of Jesus Christ.

The most ancient part of Liss is the area around Liss Place, once called Place House and formerly an ancient nunnery. It is still possible to find traces of the ancient refectory and curious fluted chimneys, although the building was considerably altered in the nineteenth century. Mrs Bashford's All About Lyss (1922) contains a picture of Place House taken from an old painting. Mrs Bashford refers to part of the house that used to be called Castle End and says it is different architecturally and is 'reputed to be haunted'.

Once there was an avenue of trees leading to Lyss Place, where a certain Dame Cole was in the habit of driving her coach-in-hand of black horses and a ghostly coach-and-four has repeatedly been seen and heard here over the years, and there are stories of phantom monks and nuns. The late Colonel Doxford used to talk about a ghost nun at the back of the house and of occasionally seeing groups of ghost nuns and monks.

I talked with a number of local people who had first-hand knowledge of Lyss Place and they all knew about the ghostly coach and horses and the phantom forms of monks and nuns that have haunted the area for hundreds of years.

About thirty-five years ago, during the Second World War, country folk were encouraged to keep livestock to help the war effort and in respect of pigs, it was permitted to keep one out of four for personal use, each year. At that time Mr Fry, who still lives at Liss, now in his eightieth year, kept the shop next to the garage at that time and four pigs. The time came when he was to have his pigs slaughtered and he and a friend went to see Dick Whittington at Hawkley to make arrangements for the killing.

It was a cold December evening, frosty but bright moonlight and as they walked along the road past Lyss Place they both saw a figure walking across the fields towards them, on their left. It seemed that it would meet them except that a trimmed hedge bordered the road. Somewhat puzzled by the figure out in the fields on such a cold night, they saw as it drew nearer that it was a monk in a brown habit, with the cowl drawn up to cover the head against the bitter cold.

Sure enough it reached the road they were travelling a little way ahead of them and to their surprise it did not stop at the hedge and it did not climb over — it simply passed through the hedge without a sound or causing any movement of the dense hedge. Then the figure seemed to come to rest on the grass verge at the side of the road — and then, suddenly, it was not there! Both men saw it, they never forgot it, and they never discovered any explanation.

LYMINGTON

The Angel, formerly the George, is a well-known hostelry in the High Street that has long been reputed to be haunted. There was an inn here in the sixteenth century; it became the Angel in the middle of the seventeenth century and then stagecoaches brought a new prosperity to this historic and delightful building that today caters no less superbly for the modern traveller.

As befits a former coaching inn a ghostly coachman haunts the place. He is a shadowy figure, most frequently seen very early in the morning, standing near the kitchen window and seemingly looking out into the yard, waiting perhaps for the arrival of the coach that he is due to drive.

Standing as it does on the estuary of the river Boldre, Lymington has many naval memories and associations and it is only right and proper that the Angel should also have a naval ghost. He is a tall, grey-haired man, wearing a long coat with brass buttons. A relief manager saw him one night at 11.30 and when he related his experience, he learned that others had seen the same silent, still figure that seemed to be there one minute and gone the next.

One visitor, in 1966, occupied a bedroom that adjoined the old assembly hall where many grand balls took place a hundred years ago. On the first night at the Angel she complained of loud piano playing long after midnight; really loud, as though someone was thumping the piano keys with all his might. The manager told her that the only piano in the establishment was long disused and beyond repair and had in fact been removed only the day before and broken up. This visitor happened to be the sister-in-law of the then manager and there can be no doubt that she had heard a piano being played with great gusto — as doubtless had been the case many years before — but now there was no piano...

MARCHWOOD

Here the old naval magazine was reputedly haunted by a Highland soldier. One night, around Christmas time, the officer-of-the-guard on duty was surprised to hear the sound of a shot. The sergeant could not explain the matter although he too had heard the shot. Next night two shots were heard and this time there was an explanation. A sentry said he had seen a soldier in the uniform of a Highland regiment coming towards him. He had challenged the figure twice and receiving no reply, had fired point blank at the figure. The shot had no effect and the Highlander continued to approach so the sentry tried again and again the shot had no effect. The figure was by this time almost upon the sentry so he tried the cold steel of his bayonet. The blade passed through the figure without resistance and the sentry fainted.

There is a story that years before a Highland soldier was told that he had to go on duty at Marchwood over the Christmas holiday instead of having leave, as he had hoped and expected and planned. Full of unhappiness and the injustice of this world, he had committed suicide in the river. The ghost is one that has some sort of official recognition in as much as it was long the practice for the authorities to enquire about the ghost having been seen over Christmas periods, and several entries are duly recorded, mostly followed by the terse comment, 'Not seen'.

MEONSTOKE

Full of old, mellow houses, this charming village is also full of mysteries. A curious hoard of hidden treasure was found here in 1441 when 'a great multitude of rats' fell into the malt-room of the parsonage and during the rat hunt that followed the servants found a large number of gold nobles. The money was at first claimed by the Crown but when a 'tempest of wind' blew down five houses, Henry VI wrote to the Lord Chancellor and Rector Thomas Wassille was permitted to keep the find.

The burial register records the death of one Elizabeth Erwaker on 10 December, 1778, adding beneath the entry, 'fell dead on appealing to God in confirmation of a lie'. We seek in vain to discover the story behind that line but perhaps it is a warning to us all.

Meonstoke House is a motley of architecture with parts dating back to 1713, a wing added in 1870 and later additions in the first decade of the twentieth century. It is possible that some of the prosperous country gentlemen who occupied the house over the years may not have been as honourable and respectable as they seemed, especially perhaps in the eighteenth century when it could be that something happened that left behind a curious atmosphere that is especially susceptible to dogs. In the village it is well known that for as long as living memory no one has been able to keep a dog at Meonstoke House.

Alen and Valerie Warner and their two children had no knowledge of this when they moved into the house in November 1975, together with an old English Sheepdog that had always behaved well in strange houses but no sooner was she taken into Meonstoke House than she became very agitated, darting to and fro and seeming to be worried and unable to settle. As the days passed her behaviour continued to puzzle its owners. During the hours of daylight she would constantly try to get out of the house and when she was outside she did nothing but howl. At night, she seemed to spend the hours of darkness restlessly padding round the house, whining. In the huge hall she was especially affected and when no part of the house seemed to suit her and she was obviously unhappy and not going to settle in the house, the family reluctantly decided to part with their family pet. Within a few days, in a strange farmhouse with strange people, she was completely happy. Later a local man told Alen Warner that 'no one has ever been able to keep a dog there — they all go wild...'

Other curious incidents experienced by the Warners at Meonstoke House have included the front door bell ringing of its own accord. This has happened so often and in such circumstances that it seems quite impossible that the ringing could be the result of human beings... and then there is the small door on the first landing that refuses to stay closed at night.

In the recent incidents that have been reported at Meonstoke House perhaps we are seeing the remnants of a haunting that has never come to light.

NETTLESTONE NEAR RYDE, ISLE OF WIGHT

The Blue Lady portrait

Galleon World Travel Associates acquired The Priory Hotel and its ghosts in 1938. This fascinating house has an equally fascinating ghost story and historic associations that still retain a few mysteries.

There is for instance a persistent legend that an

underground passage runs from the Priory to the old Farmhouse that once stood on part of the extensive lands granted to the monks soon after the Norman Conquest. The house takes its name from Saint Helen's Priory that once stood in the field behind the present cottages. No remains exist of the original cell that belonged to the Cluniac Order in Burgundy and today the house has an individual charm that reflects the love and care of succeeding owners ever since the days when it was a farmhouse. Over the years it has grown into a fine mansion, beautifully situated among trees and flower beds and with lawns sweeping towards the blue sea.

Everywhere there are memories of days gone by. There is the superb Tudor fireplace in the great entrance hall; Jacobean oak panelling in the lounge; the seventeenth century gold thread embroidered curtains; and, behind the Tithe Barn, once used by farmers and their hay wagons, a large flat stone is said to commemorate a fortunate or divine deliverance from the wrath of the elements. A hundred years or so ago a visitor to the Priory was relaxing in the sun on this spot when a thunderstorm suddenly broke. He fled for cover leaving his deck chair to be rescued later — but it was not to be, even as he reached shelter the spot where he had been sitting seconds earlier was struck by lightning and the deck chair was turned to ashes before his eyes!

But the real interest at the Priory Hotel is the ghost story for which I am indebted to Kenneth Lee of Galleon World Travel Association who is now resident at the house and to my friend Mrs Sheila White of Saint Helens. It is a story involving a lost portrait and a stuffed dog.

The monks enjoyed their estates at Saint Helens for many years but during the reign of Henry V all foreign religious orders were banished from England and the Priory lands lapsed to the Crown. Henry VI granted the revenues of Eton College and during the reign of Edward IV the lands were granted to the bursars of Eton College as a thank-offering on the occasion of his marriage to Elizabeth Wordville. The estate remained in the ownership of Eton College until 1799 when it was purchased by Sir Grose Nash, a judge and founder of the Grose-Smith family who built the main block of the mansion much as it survives to this day.

The Grose-Smiths lived at the Priory into the late 1920s when the house passed for a short time to a man who was the victim of a financial disaster; it then passed into the hands of a very wealthy American lady who associated herself with England's Patron Saint and adopted the Saint and the Dragon as her symbol and even changed her name to Saint George.

Mrs St George made many interesting improvements to both the house and grounds; the curious front porch is just one reminder of her ownership. It is certainly older than the rest of this section of the house and probably dates from the fourteenth century. Mrs St George acquired the porch in France and had it rebuilt at the Priory, stone by stone, adding a sculptured figure of St George and the Dragon in a different stone. On the death of Mrs St George in 1938 the property passed to Galleon Travel Association. After opening for a short season in 1939 it was occupied by the Army during the Second World War and reopened as an hotel in 1946.

For some years during the hundred-and-thirty year occupation of the Grose-Smiths, from 1799 until 1927, there hung in the dining-room of the house a charming portrait of a young girl with a little pointed face, half-smiling, with a canary perched on one hand and a bright-eyed little dog playing at her feet. No one seems to know who it represents but it was always known in the family as 'The Blue Lady', the child being portrayed in a deep blue dress. Mrs Sheila White is a descendant of the Grose-Smiths and she has recalled for me visiting the house as a child and falling in love with the beautiful old house and being particularly impressed by the full-length portrait of The Blue Lady. The child portrayed seems to be about fourteen years of age and there was always a story that she died soon after the portrait was finished. There is good evidence that her ghost has been seen in the grounds of The Priory and in the road and fields nearby, sometimes playing with a little dog as she must have done so often in her short life.

The dog was stuffed after its death and Mrs

White still remembers being a little frightened of the life-like creature in the glass case over the stairs, its bright eyes seeming to follow her movements. As a child she can remember thinking that it would bark at any moment.

Soon after the house changed hands Mrs White, her mother and her grandmother called to meet the enigmatic Mrs St George. Almost the first question she asked of those ladies whose family had owned the house for generations was, 'Is the place haunted?' The future Mrs White then heard first-hand the many strange experiences from the lips of the new owner. The first thing she had noticed was the considerable difficulty she had in keeping servants; first one would give notice and then another; a replacement would be found, only to leave very shortly after he, or she, had apparently settled in and was quite happy and comfortable: it was all very puzzling for the new owner who could get no satisfactory answer to her questions as to the reason for the constant change of servants. And then the butler gave notice. He had been at the house for over twenty years and Mrs St George interviewed him and insisted on knowing why he wanted to leave. And then it came out: 'Well, madam, we can't stand stand the noises at night. We hear a girl running along the corridor, sobbing and calling for her dog. It's really heartrending...'

Apparently whenever one of the staff, hearing the noises for the first time, went to see what was happening, all was immediately quiet and there was nothing to be seen; although on occasions some of the servants, including the hardened butler, claimed to have heard the soft, childlike footsteps actually run past them and their eyes would follow the sounds — but one can take only so much of that sort of thing, explained the butler to his astonished new mistress, who began to wonder just what kind of a house she had bought!

Mrs St George was an astute judge of character and she had no doubt that her butler was telling the truth; indeed, his story could explain the mysterious and continual changing of staff but Mrs St George wanted independent evidence and she began to make enquiries herself among the local people and she soon discovered that a ghostly girl did indeed haunt the old house and the immediate surrounding area — but they knew nothing of any ghost dog. According to everyone Mrs St George spoke to who claimed to have seen the ghost girl or knew anything about her, there was no ghost dog accompanying the phantom girl.

At length Mrs St George talked to an old gardener who had worked on the estate for many years and he mentioned a stuffed dog that had resided for as long as he could remember in a glass case over the stairs. Now it was gone, sold with much of the original contents of the old house. Could the presence of this stuffed dog have any connection with the portrait of the girl in blue, the ghost girl perhaps; and if so could the removal of the stuffed dog cause the ghost to appear in some way — and if the stuffed dog could be found and returned to its original place, would the haunting become less disturbing? All these and other questions flew into Mrs St George's fertile imagination as she listened to the old gardener describe the little stuffed dog in its glass case and the antique dealers who were present at the sale of the house contents and who might well have bought the dog.

It seemed to Mrs St George that there was unlikely to be a very great demand for such an object and she put an advertisement in an Island newspaper without delay. To her delight she received an answer, she found the stuffed dog still for sale in an antique shop, bought it for the princely sum of £1 and bore it back in triumph to her home, confident that the restoration of the stuffed dog to its rightful place would bilk the ghost.

Having ascertained exactly where the object had rested for many years, Mrs St George gave instructions for the stuffed dog to be replaced and there it remains to this day — and there have been no further reports of the ghost dog being seen or heard and most of the apparently paranormal noises ceased. Indeed, Mr Kenneth Lee tells me that once someone, unaware of the story, removed the stuffed dog and put it in the cellar and almost immediately strange noises were heard throughout the house at night. The dog was quickly replaced and the noises ceased.

The ghost girl, the Blue Lady of Nettlestone, may still walk occasionally and in fact she has been seen in recent years but now she walks, quietly and seemingly content; there is no running and no crying and no calling for her lost dog.

To complete the story and perhaps placate or even lay the ghost it would be nice to be able to report the restoration of the portrait of the Blue Lady to the Priory but the picture was inherited by Commander Douglas, R.N. (retired) and it now hangs at his home in Sussex. Who knows, perhaps one day it will return to its original home and then perhaps the ghost of a little girl will walk no more.

NEW FOREST

There are many stories of fairies and little people being seen in parts of the New Forest; usually they are seen only for a split second, out of the corner of the eye but seemingly quite distinct and quite inexplicable. And there are areas where 'something' invisible affects wild beasts and mankind.

There was the case of the cyclist touring the forest and calmly pedalling his way along a road overshadowed by trees when suddenly a great surge of fear swept over him. The hair on the back of his neck stood up, his brow beaded with perspiration and he felt a heavy weight press on him. He was a very unimaginative and down-to-earth character but that strange incident remained with him for the rest of his life; a sense of fear that completely overwhelmed him. What could have caused such a feeling?

Another man and a friend, equally stable and level-headed, saw something in the Forest that was very frightening. It happened in thick fog and perhaps that may have been part of the explanation but the people who were present did not think so. They were walking in the middle of the road because of the dense fog and aware of the utter silence. They had been walking for some time and were as happy as anyone would be in those circumstances. They were chatting normally and certainly not thinking about ghosts or ghostly happenings.

Suddenly they became aware of the sound of hoofbeats behind them and of the bustle and flurry that accompanies a pack of hounds and horses. The sounds quickly approached them and aware that there was a deep ditch on one side of the road and a thick hedge on the other side, the walkers stood rooted in their tracks, undecided what to do. The next moment great misty figures, horses, riders and hounds, seemed to envelope them and pass over them and then, away ahead of them, the sounds quickly died away. Had a phantom hunt really passed them, leaving no trace? The two friends continued on their way; silent, stunned, bemused; aware that something had happened that they were totally unable to explain and conscious of the deep mystery of the Forest on certain nights.

Another pair of travellers in the Forest, on a different road, years later, on a bright moonlit night, saw something they could never explain. Ahead of them they saw a large man walking towards them. As they drew nearer they both thought how oddly he was dressed for he seemed to be wearing a caped coat that suggested the Georgian era. The traveller passed and they thought no more about the big man. And then, presently, and to their astonishment, they saw the same man ahead of them again, walking towards them! It seemed quite impossible that he could have made a detour and got in front of them but, again noting his strange appearance, they passed without comment. A few miles further on the same thing happened yet again. This time they determined to address the strange figure but before they could do so he was suddenly upon them and had passed by. They looked at each other and prepared to step in the path of the odd figure and ask some directions when next they encountered him, but they never saw the man, if man it was, again and the episode has become one more inexplicable incident recorded in the New Forest.

There is also a strange story of a groaning tree in the Forest. The tree seemed to groan like a dying man and scientists and practical students of trees visited the tree, situated in the south of the Forest, but no mundane explanation seemed to fill the bill. It wasn't the wind for the groaning was heard on still nights and in winter and summer. Scraping boughs was not the answer... finally the tree was cut down and the authorities and the scientists combined to find an explanation but they never did find one.

Rufus Stone, where King William II of England met his death, is said to be haunted by the unquiet spirit of the Norman King and certainly there is room for speculation in the manner of his death. The traditional story tells of the King and his party, including his brother Henry, Baron Robert Fitz-

Hamnon, Walter Tirel of Poix, William of Breteuil, Earl Gilbert and his brother Roger of the house of Clare, splitting up once they were in the woods and waiting for the deer to be driven towards them. At sundown a stag bounded into the clearing in front of the King. He shielded his eyes and watched it through the trees. He let fly an arrow that wounded the animal and as he was so engaged Walter Tirel unintentionally shot the King in the chest. The King said not a word but in attempting to remove the arrow, broke off the shaft and then fell upon the wound and so accelerated his death. An alternative version suggests that the arrow glanced off an oak tree and struck the King. And there are whispers that it was no accident at all. What is certain is that all the hunters fled and Walter Tirel, the shoes of his horse reversed, made at once for the coast where he embarked immediately for Normandy. Henry went straight to Winchester to claim the crown and William of Breteuil followed to claim it for the eldest son, Robert, then in the Holy Land. The dead King was abandoned and Rufus' body lay where it fell until a charcoal-burner named Purkis found it and took it to Winchester in his farm cart.

It is said that the body oozed blood all the way and on the anniversary of the death on 2 August, 1100, the restless ghost of Rufus follows the same bloody trail from Castle Malwood Walk to Winchester. At the same time Ocknell Pond, to the west of Rufus Stone, is said to turn blood red in memory of

Walter Tirel washing his guilty hands.

ODIHAM

Odiham Castle ruins

The crumbling, ruined castle known to David, son of Robert the Bruce, Henry I and Queen Elizabeth, will always be associated with King John, for it was from here that he set out for Runnymede in 1203 and it was here that he returned — probably in the vilest of tempers. When I asked the way to the ruin one summer day in 1980 the local inhabitant replied, 'Oh, you mean King John's Castle...' But it is no ghost of king or knight or even a man-at-arms that haunts this almost vanished ruin but the ghost of a long forgotten wandering minstrel. On still, moonlit autumn evenings the clear notes of some piping instrument have been heard, a snatch of some vigorous tune hangs for a moment in the quiet air and, more rarely, the form of a wandering minstrel, that 'thing of shreds and patches' has been glimpsed among the age-old stones. Many people, among them my late friend Mrs Alasdair Alpin MacGregor (who presented us with a young maple tree when we moved to Hampshire), have heard music and experienced strange feelings near the old castle.

In August, 1980, I talked with an old inhabitant of Greywell, Ted, who is over eighty and has always lived in this delightful little village along the canal from Odiham Castle. He told me that during his young days there were tales of the prisoners at Odiham castle in years long past, coming out of the ruins on moonlit nights. In particular he recalled some young men who had walked from Odiham along the bank of the canal and as they had passed the castle they always said they had seen figures coming out of the ruins, dressed in clothing of a bygone age and making not a sound...

Odiham is a pleasant old town with its wide main street, reminiscent of coaching days and it has an animal ghost. A phantom black dog is reputed to run at unspecified times down the High Street and out of the town. One wonders what story lies behind this ghost; what event caused this apparition or is it merely the case of a long-past event being recorded on the atmosphere in some way that we do not yet understand.

Not far from Odiham there is a Tudor Cottage where the inhabitant, who lived there for more than twenty years, told me she had no doubt whatever that the place was haunted. On many occasions she found herself suddenly wide awake in the middle of the night; overwhelmed with depression and by an awful feeling of dread and then she would hear sounds that seemed to come from the next room, including an ominous dull thud, although the room was uninhabited; indeed my informant lived quite alone, apart from the ghosts. Only once did she actually see anything. Late one evening, coming hurriedly out of the sitting room, her thoughts totally on her supper, which she thought was burning, she almost bumped into the figure of a burly man dressed as an Elizabethan peasant. She was able to describe the form minutely. He wore a sort of tunic, blue and belted, and his legs were bound with some sort of coarse cloth. Surprised, she stopped in her tracks and turned to watch him as he moved towards the sitting-room door — where he vanished.

One day she met a clairvoyant who told her, quite spontaneously and before she had spoken a dozen words to him, that she lived in a haunted house, where a man had murdered his wife in Tudor times (the 'thud', perhaps?) and afterwards had hanged himself in a 'little room leading off the sitting-room'. The victim, said the clairvoyant, was buried in her native village of Crondall (which he pronounced as spelt and not the local pronunciation: Crundall) and the man was buried at the far end of the farm premises opposite the cottage. Another inexplicable sound heard in the cottage at dead of night resembled a bouncing ping-pong ball.

Following a talk about 'Ghosts' that I gave in Farnham in May, 1980, a member of the audience asked me whether I had come across a ghostly coachman on the A87 Farnham Road out of Odiham. ITer father had encountered such a figure and a few days later my wife and I went to see this gentleman who lives a few hundred yards from the scene of his curious experience.

It was dusk one evening in June, 1978 when my informant, Mr Latham, was travelling home to Bo-wood, as he had done scores of times before, thinking of nothing in particular and certainly not of coachmen or ghosts, when suddenly, at a spot where some ancient trees border the road, he saw a man ahead standing at the side of the road. The figure was dressed in a long, old-fashioned coat, he wore a three-cornered hat, gaiters and shoes with big brass buckles. A moment later the figure stepped out into the road and then the feet and lower part of the legs seemed to disappear. He carried what appeared to be a pair of long gloves over one arm.

At this point Mr Latham was in some difficulty in relating the rest of the experience. He had certainly stopped the car, thinking that the figure was a man who was attending some sort of fancy dress function and needed a lift. He wound down his passenger window and waited, but the figure did not speak, yet the puzzled motorist seemed to sense that the figure was asking a question, something like: 'Has the coach left the turnpike?' The next moment the figure had completely disappeared and the road and roadside and clump of trees were totally deserted.

Looking back on the experience, and in answer to my questions, I learned from Mr Latham that the colour of the long coat had appeared to be dark green with black or dark buttons and there was a crest of some kind on the dome-shaped buttons. The man also carried a whip. The coat was the sort that had a short shoulder cape and it seemed to be fastened at the top with a short chain.

Two things may or may not be related to this remarkably vivid episode, the only one of its kind ever experienced by the recipient: a few years earlier an Army serviceman, his wife and their child were in a car that swung off the road at this exact point, and crashed into a tree; the car burst into flames and all the occupants were killed. Had the driver seen and tried to avoid a similar figure to that seen by Mr Latham? Secondly, the surface of the present road at this point was raised when the road was rebuilt; originally the road had been a foot or so lower. Could this account for the disappearance of the legs of the figure when it went into the road? Neither of these facts, either the building-up of the road or the fatal accident, were known to my informant at the time he saw the phantom coachman looking for his coach that never comes.

PORTCHESTER NEAR FAREHAM

Portchester Castle

The Castle, situated by the northern extremity of Portsmouth Harbour and the waterway's natural guardian, was built by the Romans and although it is now nothing but a shell, enclosing some nine acres, it is still the most extensive and complete remnant of Roman architecture in these islands. The air about those massive walls seems to breathe history and so they might. King John remodelled some parts, Richard II others; Henry I others again; Edward II began the beautiful porch and Edward III completed it and stayed here before embarking for Crecy; Henry VIII and Anne Boleyn stayed here while hawking ; and it is even said that nearby Paulsgrove gets its name from Saint Paul the Apostle disembarking here to continue his ministrations and that Pontius Pilate, when he was very old and troubled by his conscience, was brought to Portchester Castle in one of the Roman galleys.

Of course Portchester Castle has a ghost although it does not appear to have been described in any great detail by those fortunate, or unfortunate, enough to have seen it. 'A tall, whitish object' is about as far as most of the witnesses will go in describing what they have seen. Often it seems to appear suddenly in a dark corner. Two very practical people saw the ghostly shape independently on the same day at an interval of some hours but by all accounts the appearances are irregular. It is generally accepted as being the ghost of a prisoner who said he would return after death.

There has been the suggestion that the Portchester Castle Ghost originated in an uninvited actor, at a time when the authorities occasionally permitted theatrical performances to be held there in the eighteenth century, suddenly putting in an appearance, apparently from nowhere, and as mysteriously disappearing.

Telford Varley, writing on Hampshire in 1908, describes Portchester Castle perfectly— '. . .formerly a busy spot, a fortress and a seaport, it is now little more than a memory of the past. Yet by the wide, sad stretch of inland water, mud and ooze and flapping water-weed, Portchester ruins still keep solemn watch, like some ghost of bygone ages guarding the scene of former achievements...'

PORTSMOUTH

The old Spotted Dog, a famous inn of Portsmouth, where John Felton murdered the Duke of Buckingham in 1628, was long said to be haunted by the sounds of murder and the fleeting glimpse of a man in seventeenth century clothes, dashing out of one of the rooms. An obelisk on Clarence Pier marks the place where the murderer was displayed in chains.

Did the ghost of Charlie Matthews, lost in the L24 submarine disaster, return to his home in Portsmouth? Charlie had a premonition that he would not return from manoeuvres off the south coast that day in 1924 but he was one of the crew of the submarine and he tearfully told his wife that he had to go, although he knew he would not come back. The boat will come up,' he told his wife, 'And then go down and when we come up again we will be struck by something and that will be the end of us...' So miserable did he feel, so certain that he would not see his wife again that he did not sleep at all the night before he had to report for duty.

A few days later, in their home, Mrs Matthews distinctly heard her husband's voice call her name. Overjoyed at the thought that he had returned safely, she turned round, exclaiming, 'Is that you,

Charlie?' There was nobody there. At the precise moment that Mrs Matthews had this experience, which she never forgot, Mrs Dicks, who was staying in the same house, heard the voice of Charlie Matthews say, 'Look after her...'

By that time the submarine L24 had met disaster and sunk. The circumstances surrounding the event, according to expert opinion, were exactly as foreseen by the drowned sailor.

The old Theatre Royal has long been reputed to be haunted by the ghost of John Ruttley, actor-manager at the theatre from 1866 to 1874, who shot himself in the dressing room that carried his name. People who used the dressing room often complained of unusual sensations, strange noises such as whisperings and sighs, and the presence of some unseen being.

Soon after a rock and roll club opened in a room situated immediately above the haunted John Ruttley dressing room in 1958, two young art students and the club vocalist Shane Shaw, asked the theatre director Robert Stigwood whether they might have a look at the old dressing room.

As he let them into the room, telling them something of the history of the theatre at the same time, the lights were suddenly switched off, the door slammed and they all heard footsteps walking up and down the corridor outside although they were alone in the building at the time.

'We knew there was no one else in the theatre,' Robert Stigwood said at the time. 'But we carefully looked out and there was no one there. We thought it was time we went home... I turned off the lights in the corridor. But I had gone only about six steps when the lights clicked on again, although no one was near the switch.' The theatre general manager, Geoffrey Wren, also reported hearing the ghostly footsteps in the deserted building on more than one occasion. He wondered whether the staid John Ruttley objected to the modern music and dancing and was showing his displeasure...

A curious story was once told to the Revd R.H. Barham by Mrs Hughes, grandmother of the author of Tom Brown's Schooldays, who said she had heard the story from the wife of a man well known to her husband, Captain Hastings: a naval officer by the name of Hamilton.

According to Hamilton's story he came across an inn called The Admiral Collingwood in a quiet street of Portsmouth when he was looking for a night's lodging. Only one double room was available and it was suggested that he might like to share the room; not wishing to do so, Hamilton offered to pay the double room price if he could have the room to himself. So it was arranged but in the middle of the night he awoke to find to his astonishment (for he had carefully locked the door) that the other bed was clearly occupied by a young sailor. Furious but tired, Hamilton returned to sleep. In the morning the form was still occupying the other bed in his room and he carefully examined the still figure, especially noting the black side-whiskers before he saw a deep wound at the side of the forehead that seemed to be still bleeding and had marked the pillow. He could hear no sound of breathing nor see any movement in the still form and he decided to wake the man and demand an explanation. As he approached the bed, the figure suddenly vanished: one moment it was there, the next it had gone, and a vacant bed met his astonished gaze.

The landlady at the inn was adamant that no one had occupied the room apart from Hamilton himself but when he described the figure he had seen she became very disturbed and explained that a couple of nights previously a quarrel had broken out between three sailors staying at the inn and one had been hit on the side of the head and carried upstairs by his companions. The victim had prominent black side-whiskers. Soon afterwards the two sailors came and told her that their companion was dead. They threatened the landlady with violence unless they were allowed to bury the body in the garden and leave without her saying anything about the matter. She, mindful of the reputation of the inn, had reluctantly agreed. So it was done. Having heard this incredible story Hamilton paid his dues and left the inn.

Some years later, when he was again in Portsmouth, Hamilton was sharing a carriage with Captain and Mrs Hastings and he told them the strange experience. Next day the three set out to find The Admiral Collingwood but no such inn could they find. Where Hamilton was certain the hostelry had stood was a greengrocer's shop. The one fact that might have been regarded as substantiating Hamilton's story was the fact that they learned that the greengrocery property had been converted into a shop some five years earlier.

Nearby Fort Cumberland has long been said to be haunted by the ghost of a spy in the Napoleonic wars. My friend Dorothea St Hill Bourne has kindly related to me something of the ghost story and her memories of a visit there: 'Just after the last war I was the guest of the then Commander and his wife, old friends of mine. It was quite an experience staying in the grim, isolated old building with the waters of the Solent lapping almost all round it, especially as I and the C.O.'s wife were the only women in a wholly male community of some thousands of Marine commandos in training.

'I was told that the Fort was haunted and that the ghost was said to be that of a spy in the Napoleonic Wars who was hanged on the square outside the Commander's lodgings.

'I remember feeling rather shivery as I prepared for bed and somehow it was reassuring when I peeped from my bedroom window to see a solid, flesh-and-blood sentry on duty just below.

'One evening a young officer, newly arrived at the Fort, was asked to dine with the C.O. During dinner our hostess remarked suddenly, "Oh Captain Brown, I believe your room is in the haunted block." I remember seeing a rather bleak look cross the young man's face, which paled quite perceptibly. I thought: "At least there is something that can put the wind up a Marine Commando!"

'Nothing ghostly was seen or heard during my visit but, soon after my return home, I had a letter from the C.O.'s wife. She told me that I would be amused to hear that the ghost had been too much for Captain Brown. While sitting in the Mess he distinctly heard footsteps going upstairs and someone entering his room just overhead. As there had been some pilfering of late he thought he had caught the culprit red-handed. He dashed upstairs and into his room — to find no one there or on that floor, and everything untouched. After this had happened more than once he asked to be transferred to another part of the building. This was arranged and his old room was left unoccupied.

'A few days later the empty room was found to be on fire and serious consequences were narrowly averted. No reasonable cause for the fire was ever discovered and its origin remained a mystery.

'Did the angry spy, having evicted the tenant, find means of getting his own back on the forces of the establishment which had taken his life more than a century ago? Although I never actually saw or heard anything supernatural when I was in the Fort I was very much aware of the somewhat sinister atmosphere hanging over parts of the old building. Is this to be wondered at when one considers its past history?'

QUARR ABBEY NEAR RYDE, ISLE OF WIGHT

Here, where a grey ruined wall is all that remains of old Quarr Abbey, consecrated by Henry de Blois eight hundred years ago, a Feast of Fools took place each New Year's Day. Directed by a 'Lord of Misrule' the monks would dress up as women and conduct themselves 'undecorously', eating puddings and sausages off the altar, singing bawdy songs and burning old shoes for incense: in time the pagan Saturnalia and Bacchanalia became Christianized and today a new Abbey, built by French monks with red bricks, is one of the sights of the Island.

Tradition has it that nearby Eleanor's grove is named after Henry II's queen and mother of Richard the Lionheart. She stirred her sons to rebellion and is reputed to have been restrained at Old Quarr Abbey for many years, often taking lonely walks through the grove that now bears her name. It is said that she came to love the place and when she died her body was brought to Quarr, enclosed in a coffin of solid gold and buried at the end of an underground passage in her favourite spot among the trees that had been her silent companions for so many unhappy years. A golden gate, sealed by magic spells, marked the grave, which became lost over the years.

The story goes that in Victorian times a tomb was in fact located here and although no gold was found, the remains of an important female were unearthed. For centuries, the legend says, the ghost of the dead queen has walked among these trees.

The present secretary of Quarr Abbey tells me that he has considerable doubts about the whole story. 'A golden door and a golden coffin would be more than Henry II possessed. An underground passage in these parts would be permanently flooded and, in any case, there is no historical evidence that Queen Eleanor was buried at Quarr.' Then who is the ghostly lady who walks sadly through Eleanor's Grove?

RINGWOOD

Dick Sheppard, Public Relations Manager to the Borough of Bournemouth, tells me that a four-hundred-year-old property in Southampton Road, Ringwood, known as The Cottage, has a friendly ghost. The lady of the house says that when she retires to bed and closes the door of the first floor bedroom, she often hears a noise, like the rustling of a silk skirt along the passage and then there is a fumbling at the door as though someone is trying to enter. Some afternoons, when she has been in the same bedroom, for the purpose of having a rest or taking a nap, she has distinctly felt the presence of a friendly lady in the room who seems to be watching over her in a motherly and kindly manner. Because she is convinced that the ghost is friendly, she will not have the house exorcised.

Ebenezer Lane is reputed to be haunted by two ghosts, a Georgian lady and gentleman. Some years ago two children who lived there became accustomed to seeing the two figures which they described in some detail to their parents and although on occasions the children tried to introduce the ghost, the parents could not see what was obviously very clear and vivid to the children.

Nearby Elizabethan Moyles Court, now a school,

was once the home of Lady Alicia Lisle. Once she had been the wife of one of Cromwell's lords and records state that 'her blood leaped within her to see the tyrant fall'. She was a forceful lady who later changed her allegiance and became a staunch Royalist and although by this time a woman of advanced age, she did not hesitate when approached for sanctuary by two exhausted fugitives from Monmouth's defeated rebel army at Monmouth.

Someone talked and Royalist troopers found the men at Moyles Court. One was hiding in the malthouse and the other in a priest's hole. Old Lady Lisle was arrested and charged with high treason. She appeared before the notorious Judge Jeffreys at Winchester who cursed and raved at the calm old lady and sentenced her to be drawn on a hurdle to the place of execution and there burnt alive — and he demanded the Sheriff prepare the execution that very afternoon. But the horrified clergy managed to get the sentence postponed for five days and by that time James the Second had agreed to change the penalty to death by beheading and this sentence was duly carried out on the seventy-one-year-old gentlewoman on 5 September, 1685, at Winchester Market Place.

But Lady Alicia Lisle does not rest in peace. She has long been reputed to haunt Moyles Court, rustling along the corridors in a silk dress or walking in the courtyard; and a driverless coach drawn by headless horses is also said to convey her ghost along Ellingham Lane. Other reports say only the sounds of a carriage are heard these days, galloping up to the front entrance of the house. And her ghost has been seen, if we are to believe the reports, carrying her head under her arm, at Dibden, fifteen miles away, where her son had a house which she visited shortly before her arrest.

ROWLANDS CASTLE

Once upon a time when there were giants in these lands, Angoulaffe the Terrible plagued and pestered and troubled the people of Hampshire until one Roland became the hero of the day and slew the mighty giant, so giving his name to Rowlands Castle where, according to legend, this incident took place.

Here there is a ghost known as Charlie Pearce, a local character whose cottage is still inhabited but his ghost haunted the woods where he died. Charlie was fond of strong liquor and the story goes that one day, while inebriated, he mounted his horse and rode through the woods that now border the rectory garden. In his carelessness an overhanging branch caught him by the throat and he was plucked from his horse and throttled.

At irregular intervals over the years, at various times of daylight and darkness, the ghost of Charlie Pearce has been encountered in the woods where he met his unexpected death. The wife of a former rector has related her experience when she saw the ghost just before Christmas as she was exercising her dog and collecting evergreens for decoration.

'In the distance I suddenly saw a rider dressed

in a fawn coat, on horseback. I looked away for some reason and then when I looked again, he was nowhere to be seen.' When she reached the spot where the figure had appeared she realised that the thick undergrowth and overgrown shrubs and thick bushes could not possibly have allowed access for a real horse and rider. Furthermore the behaviour of her dog suggested that he sensed something not of this world. 'He stopped dead in his tracks, shook all over, and would not move forward. Eventually I told him to go home and he turned and fled back the way we had come. When I got home I found him waiting at the back door of the rectory, still shaking like a leaf.'

A few months later, in the same area of woodland, the dog acted in a similar way, causing its owner to think that again it saw or sensed something that it could not understand. On that occasion its mistress saw nothing.

RYE COMMON NEAR CRONDALL

Here there are vague but persistent rumours of a phantom coach and one wonders whether there can be any connection between this apparition and the ghostly coaches associated with Itchel Manor, Jenkyn Place, Bentley Crossroads, the Lion and Lamb and the Hop Bag Inn at Farnham, all nearby.

One person I talked to seemed to consider it significant that all the reports seemed to relate to wintry nights and he thought the crisp, clear air of winter might be conducive to certain ghostly appearances.

One of the few witnesses of the ghost coach of Rye Common that I have been able to trace said that the coach had appeared suddenly, without any warning and without making any sound, and almost as soon as he was able to take in the startling sight of the old-fashioned, rocking coach, racing away ahead of him, the whole thing had disappeared as mysteriously as it had appeared. There have also been a number of reports of animals suddenly showing fright for no apparent reason in the area and one wonders whether they have sensed something not perceived by human beings and that on occasions the coach is invisible.

SELBORNE

The village that saw the birth and death of Gilbert White, the naturalist who produced one book, The Natural History of Selborne, and made this still largely unspoilt village a place of pilgrimage. One of Gilbert White's gifts to generations of visitors to Selborne is the Zig Zag, a tortuous climb of steps up his beloved Hanger, the steep hill behind the village where, at the top, you will find a wishing stone. But if you want your wish to come true you must walk blindfold backwards round the stone three times and then sit on the stone and wish.

And it is here in the Hanger that we meet the first of Selborne's ghosts for up here amid the tall trees and ferns and flowers that meant so much to Gilbert White there have been reports from responsible people who say they have seen nonhuman forms. Sometimes these forms are human size, sometimes — especially it seems when they are seen by children — they are smaller than human beings.

Mrs Brian Vesey-Fitzgerald told Dorothea St Hill Bourne that she had a maid who had been brought up at Selbourne. One day Mrs Vesey-Fitzgerald brought home a large, quaint figure of a gnome in a pointed cap. The maid saw it and said, 'Oh madam, that's just like the little men we used to see on Selbourne Hanger when we were children. Mother said we told stories because she could not see them, but we children could...'

Selbourne Priory had a brief and inglorious history, being dissolved in 1484. Some fascinating information and physical relics are preserved in Gilbert White's old home, now a museum. The last but one Prior of Selborne was named John Sharpe and the Priory was dissolved only a couple of years after his death. In 1525 the Priory lands were leased to another John Sharpe and he and his successors (all Sharpes) farmed the land for over a hundred years. There are stories of a ghostly monk being seen in the vicinity of the long-vanished Priory and along the old road that the monks built and which is still in remarkably good repair. When excavations were taking place there were many reports of a ghost figure, a thin man with dark hair, large eyes, a sallow skin, small oval face and a long nose. The figure often had its head bowed, its chin on its chest, and most of the witnesses said there seemed to be a greyish mist round the figure that wore a black monk's habit with the cowl thrown back off the head. A Brighton woman, named Sharpe, told the Revd G. Knapp that in 1962 she saw a ghost monk who she believed was the old Prior Sharpe of Selborne.

A fifteenth century farm that once formed part of the old Priory estate has a phantom dog that often appears at the site of the original entrance to the Priory Farm. Although the people at the farm say they have not seen the ghost, former occupants and local people have been more fortunate, or unfortunate. Mr Edward Lucas always maintained that he saw the ghost dog on two occasions. Each time it was about nine o'clock in the evening and he would be taking a horse to the old harness room when, twice, he suddenly saw a strange black dog with long black hair, about the size of a collie. It seemed to appear from nowhere and walked beside Lucas and the horse for perhaps a hundred yards before suddenly and completely vanishing, not far from the old farm entrance. What surprised Edward Lucas was the fact that, if it was a ghost, the horses and his own dog were completely unaffected by the appearance; indeed they seemed not to be aware of the phantom dog.

Many years ago a number of bones were dug up in the area of the farm and the Old Priory but most of them seemed to be human bones and very ancient. A persistent local story concerning the ghost dog says it was the constant companion of one of the racehorses that used to be bred there in the nineteenth century and was accidentally killed in an accident at the farm.

The ghost monk is still encountered occasionally. I was told in 1976 that it had been seen by three walkers who were strolling along the Old Priory Road. As the figure passed them, seemingly deep in thought, they murmured a casual greeting but received no reply and indeed the figure seemed not to notice them. As soon as it had passed they turned to look at the oddly quiet and preoccupied form that they had seen, only to find the roadway completely deserted. Afterwards they realised that the figure had made no sound whatsoever. Some years before, Raymond Osborne, a great admirer of Gilbert White, had visited Selborne and then taken the little road out of the village and the walk through the woods along the Old Priory road. There he had seen, after rounding a corner, the figure of a monk in a black habit about a hundred yards ahead of him. After a little while he quickened his pace, thinking to have a word with the man but he found that however fast he walked, the monk seemed to be still the same distance ahead and then, where the woods ended with a gate into the fields leading to the Priory, the figure suddenly disappeared. Raymond Osborne, the most practical and level-headed of men, was completely mystified for there seemed no possible path the monk could have taken without being visible. He never saw another ghost but that sighting puzzled him to the end of his days.

SHANKLIN, ISLE OF WIGHT

A stone house in the old Village is called Vernon Cottage, and probably has historic connections with Admiral Edward Vernon, known as 'Old Grog' in the Royal Navy which he entered in 1707, and in which he subsequently saw much active service. During the long peace under Walpole he clamoured for war with Spain and declared in 1739 that he could capture Porto- bello with a squadron of six ships. He got the command and the ships, and captured Portobello with a loss of only seven men. Years later he was annoyed at the intervention from Whitehall when he was a Member of Parliament and published some of his instructions; this resulted in his being struck off the Flag List.

Whether or not the ghostly maiden long reputed to haunt the vicinity of Vernon Cottage has anything to do with Admiral Vernon is uncertain but it would appear unlikely since the Admiral died in 1757 (at Nacton in Suffolk) and the ghost maiden appears to be wearing a flowing seventeenth century dress.

I have been unable to discover the story behind the haunting but it is generally considered that the girl runs down the road from the cottage to meet a young man. The case is interesting in as much as this would appear to be a daylight ghost. It could be that the story stems from some tragedy associated with smugglers who once haunted the area in a very practical way. There are lots of stories about smugglers' tunnels from the chine coming out underneath some of the older properties in Shanklin.

The present Pier Theatre is, it would seem, occasionally haunted; the old Pier Theatre that once stood on the same site was certainly haunted before it was destroyed by fire.

The ghost is said to be an old-time entertainer, Albert DuBois, whose monologues delighted audiences in the 1890s. He was a tall man with white hair, he wore mutton-chop whiskers and sported a grey cravat with a diamond pin. Jon Garr, the popular local organist and entertainer, has seen such a figure and is in no doubt about the ghost. Others have seen the same form.

Apart from visual experiences Jon Garr has noticed an area of coldness on the steps from the stage to the dressing rooms and a feeling of being watched. Other performers have remarked on the same impressions and one wonders whether poor old Albert DuBois returns to the theatre to hear again the applause that is everything to a dedicated performer.

Interestingly enough one particular seat in the auditorium has also been reported to be unnaturally cold but why this should be, no one seems able to explain.

It is interesting too to learn that the present theatre has nine steps leading on to the stage whereas the old theatre had seven. Footsteps have been repeatedly heard mounting these steps as the actor or performer has heard his cue and is about to go on stage — but only seven footfalls are heard climbing the steps to the stage and they are never heard going back...

SHERFIELD ON LODDON NEAR BASINGSTOKE

Sherfield Manor

Here the former owner of the grey, fourteenth century watermill used to complain of a 'shadow' that came and stood beside him at night-time when he was stone-dressing. He said the shadow or shade was that of a tall man with a long face and a beard and the miller had the distinct impression that the presence was criticising his method of doing the work! On making enquiries he discovered that a man answering this description used to work at Lailey's Mill many years ago and that he was known far and wide as an expert stone-dresser.

Outside the village is the house once known as Sherfield Manor; now it is a school and when I called there with my grandson Toby in August,

1980, I heard something of the reputed haunting. Even today there are occasional reports from the girls that they have seen the figure of a woman in a grey dress who appears and disappears in peculiar circumstances — but most of those stories are dismissed by the staff as 'such stuff as dreams are made on'.

Not so perhaps the experience of Miss Irene Cooper-Willis, barrister-at-law, who wrote to Sir Ernest Bennett in 1937 about experiences in 1926, a letter that this Society for Psychical Research member published in his monumental Apparitions and Haunted Houses in 1939 and I am indebted to Sir Ernest's daughter Mrs Marguerite White for permission to reproduce that letter here: 'In the Spring or Summer of 1926 I was staying at Sherfield Manor, near Basingstoke. I went to bed quite early one evening, about eleven or thereabouts. In my bedroom I discovered to my disappointment that the bedside light would not switch on and off from the bed, and that I had to get out of bed to turn the light off. Feeling lazy, therefore, I did not read in bed but turned the light off before getting into bed and soon went to sleep The bed was an old-fashioned four poster and at the bottom, between the bed and the fireplace, was a settee with back and sides. I woke suddenly. Either there was a moon outside or it was very early morning for I could see faint light outside the window — the curtains weren't drawn, and I could see things in the room. I saw the figure of a woman sitting slightly sideways on the settee at the bottom of the bed, with her head in her hands. Her hair was dark and I saw a ring on the hand cupping her head. She had a grey dress on, as far as I could see, with big sleeves, I could not see her skirt for the back of the settee was higher than the bed. She sat there without moving and as I looked at her I felt frightened for though I sat bolt upright she never moved. I remembered that I could not turn the bedside light on, and I was too frightened to get out and switch on the light from the door. It seemed to me that I sat upright looking a her for at least half an hour, but my heart was beating and it is quite likely that I exaggerated the time from my first sight of her and her sudden vanishing. Suddenly she wasn't there — that's all I can say and then I immediately got out of bed, switched on the light and lay with the light on in bed until I heard a clock outside strike five and saw that daylight was on the way. I then went to sleep again.

'I slept in that room several times afterwards but never saw the lady again. My hostess knew nothing about her but she had not lived for many years in the house and has now left it.'

Sir Ernest Bennett rightly points out that one feature of peculiar interest in the narrative is the duration of the apparition. 'Miss Cooper-Willis speaks of "at least half an hour",' he says. 'And even if this estimate were halved or quartered — the percipient admits that there may have been an exaggeration — the persistence of the phantasm has no parallel in any record of a similar experience.' 'And sustained contemplation of an apparition,' he adds, 'by the percipient is something very different from the usual brevity of such experiences.'

SOUTHAMPTON

In 1967, soon after the demolition of the old Indian-style Victoria Military Hospital at Netley, the City Archivist sent me information about the building and its ghosts.

Queen Victoria herself laid the foundation stone on May 19, 1856, saying as she did so that she had sanctioned the naming of the building of the Royal Victoria Hospital and she was glad to think that her 'poor brave soldiers will be more comfortably lodged' than she was herself! Nevertheless her words reflected the current public opinion that the design and facilities compared favourably with the Queen's recently erected Osborne House. Later it was to become the subject of a national scandal and a War Office enquiry and to be referred to as a 'horrid example' of nineteenth century hospital construction; the first criticism came from Florence Nightingale and while it may be true that throughout its history Netley was a 'difficult, depressing and unsatisfactory hospital' as C. Woodham-Smith says in her biography of Florence Nightingale, nevertheless the building survived for over a century and catered for about a thousand patients for most of that time and in the Second World War managed to accommodate double that number.

The building was long reputed to be haunted by a nurse of the Crimean War period who committed suicide by throwing herself from an upstairs window after discovering that by mistake she had administered a fatal overdose of drugs to a patient.

Her ghost was always seen in one particular corridor. Officials and staff at the hospital, a clergyman, visitors and patients, have all told of seeing the figure, although stories of the appearances were suppressed for many years because whenever the ghost was seen, a death seemed to take place in the hospital. A service of exorcism was held there in 1951.

The apparition was reported to be particularly active when the building was being demolished and one witness stated: 'The figure was dressed in an old-style nurses' uniform of greyish-blue with a white cap and was about twenty-five feet away from me when I saw it. She walked slowly away, making no sound and disappeared down a passage that led to the chapel.'

In 1936, a night orderly saw the grey lady pass a ward where a patient died the following morning. A night staff telephone operator, employed at the hospital for twenty-seven years, also claimed to have seen the ghost; he said that he heard the rustle of her dress as she passed and there was a perfumed scent in the air after she had disappeared.

Variations of the legend suggest that the ghost was a nursing sister who fell in love with a patient and, after finding him in the arms of another nurse, poisoned him and then committed suicide. Or that the patient dies and the nurse jumped from a window because of a broken heart; or, it has been suggested, could it be Florence Nightingale herself, who was mainly responsible for the building of the hospital, and that her frequent appearances in 1966 were an endeavour to prevent its demolition.

I am indebted to a correspondent who wrote to me after reading some of my books for details of an experience that befell her in Southampton in addition to two other personal psychic experiences that have no place in this particular volume. She writes:

'At the time of the experience in Southampton I had not been very long out of College. War broke out and as my brother was working there I joined him in the August of 1940.

'At that particular time Southampton had only known the tail-end of the bombings of London, although hundreds of enemy aircraft filled the sky at times, heading north. However, as you remember, this state of affairs was to be abruptly changed. I had gone into Southampton on the Saturday afternoon to do some shopping and thought I'd go to the films at the Regal Cinema when the shopping was finished. I was living in Eastleigh at the time, which was about four or five miles outside the City. At about 4.45 p.m. I walked up the very wide steps leading into the cinema, heading for the box office. I suppose there must have been about ten steps or more and there was no one else in sight. I was carrying my shopping bag in my left hand and my handbag in my right. About halfway up the steps I was stopped abruptly by a large arm which fitted itself across my stomach at the waist, the hand holding firmly to my left side and a voice said quite clearly though not loudly, "Don't go to the pictures here, go back to Eastleigh and go to the pictures". I then became aware of a tall, well-built form standing at my right side, which appeared to be that of a man and as I was looking down at the arm which had remained across my waist, I noticed that it was muscular looking and that there were hairs on it, darkish ones. The figure wore a long, creamy, draped sort of gown with sleeves which ended at the elbow and there appeared to be a gathering or band at the waist of the gown. Naturally I thought I was 'seeing things' and my imagination was playing tricks, so I went to push against the arm and go up the steps but found that I could not move and again the voice gave the instruction for me to go back to Eastleigh and then repeated it. Never having had such an experience before, and being a pretty practical person, I just could not come to terms with what I was seeing and hearing, so I shook the sensation of the 'presence' off and again made to go up the steps. This time it did not attempt to stop me and the man gradually faded and disappeared within seconds.

After this I trotted up the steps and bought my ticket and went into the cinema. At about 6.30 p.m. ail hell broke loose, as the Germans had started their blitz on Southampton. Most of the people and myself went down into the underground toilets and sat on the stairs for several hours until things quietened down. When we same out the High Street seemed to be a mass of flames and great chunks of concrete and parts of buildings, glass and all sorts were strewn across the street — we had certainly had a plastering. We had to walk back to Eastleigh and I told the people I walked back with what had happened to me on the steps. We all agreed that something had been trying to protect me for some reason or other, anyway, we all thought it was very strange.

'After this experience, I seemed to know every time there was going to be an air raid and always knew which bombers were going over (ours or theirs) and, in addition, ever since then I have, on occasion, been conscious of voices in my head advising, or warning, of things to come and when I ignore them I always regret it.'

In 1971 two small primitive stone heads were dug up at a house in Hexham. Almost immediately strange happenings began to take place in the house where the heads reposed: strange noises and the appearance of black shapes, large and frightening, neither human nor animal... A few days after the heads had been found neighbours discovered the front door of the house burst open and the lady of the house in a confused condition; very soon she moved to another house.

The heads were sent to a large museum where they were examined before being sent to Dr Anne Ross, the prominent Southampton authority, archaeologist and expert on paganism. The small stone heads were sent from the Northern museum of antiquities without comment, for examination and report. They arrived in a small coffin-shaped box and the moment she saw the heads this practical, level-headed academic felt the most awful and intense coldness. At this stage she knew nothing whatever about the heads but she took an immediate and intense dislike to them; there seemed to be something positively evil about these two crude heads with short necks — yet this qualified, scientific specialist, who gets dozens of similar heads to examine and analyse, was shocked at the immediate impression made by these objects.

She found that she felt icy cold and very frightened. From time to time she would have a head sent to her that she didn't like, but never anything like this. She told herself she was going to analyse them and then get them out of her house as soon as possible.

There were at the time in the house five other heads which she had for examination and the stone heads were placed with the others on a chest in her study and she set to work on them. She spent three very uncomfortable days with the heads and then, three nights later, at two or three o'clock in the morning, she found herself suddenly wide awake and immediately alert in a kind of panic terror; again she became aware of extreme and unusual coldness in the normally warm bedroom and as she looked round the room, she somehow knew that a presence of some kind was in the room with her. She lay facing a window but she knew the coldness did not come from that direction and she raised herself up in bed and felt her eyes 'pulled' towards the door and there she saw a great black form, six feet high, that seemed to be half-man and half-wolf; it stood there, slightly crouched, with a canine head, a semi-human body and covered with black fur.

The upper hallway light outside the bedroom had been left switched on to comfort a little boy of five years old and as the form turned and suddenly made its way out of the bedroom and into the lighted upstairs hallway, in some strange way the startled watcher seemed to have no control over her movements and she felt impelled to follow, instead of screaming with fear and waking her sleeping husband. Dr Ross's thoughts and actions seemed temporarily controlled by some outside force and she found herself first at the bedroom door and then following the strange intruder towards the stairs. There she saw the dark shape move quickly down the stairway and when she had almost caught up with it, the form, halfway down the stairs, suddenly leapt over the banister and landed with a 'plop' — such as a padded animal might make — in the downstairs hall.

There, as she watched, full of fear but impelled by some unknown force to look and even follow, the black form turned and rushed towards the back of the house where it disappeared from view. Dr Ross ran after it, still conscious of the extreme coldness everywhere and then she suddenly stopped. The strange and frightening form had disappeared: the doors were all closed and the back door was locked... suddenly she seemed to become aware of what she was doing; she was petrified with fear but somehow she made her way back upstairs and awakened her husband, a burly, no-nonsense, practical commercial artist, and she told him what she had seen. He said he would see what was happening and despite his protests she insisted on accompanying him in a thorough search of every room in the house. They found nothing disturbed and no sign of any stray animal or intruder. The back door was still locked on the inside. Puzzled but conscious of the effect such a story might have on the children, the five-year-old boy and a fifteen-year-old girl, they decided to say nothing to either.

Next day a favourite and very intelligent black cat, Jason, was quietly sleeping, as usual, at his mistress's feet in the study while Dr Ross worked when suddenly there was a tremendous rush of wind along the hall, the study door burst open and although nothing was visible Jason, his back arched and fur bristling, backed slowly away from the open door in a strange and terrified condition. It was a long time before he went back to sleep. This kind of thing went on during the next day or two and there were strange noises...

Four days later both husband and wife had to go to London and they told the children that they would be home about six o'clock in the evening. They had a prearranged signal, a special ring on the doorbell, so that the children would know it was their parents at the door. When they arrived home, they gave their private ring on the bell and waited. After a moment the door was opened by their daughter; she was as white as a sheet and seemed to be very frightened. Her mother asked her whether she was feeling unwell and the girl replied that she had been feeling rather faint, but she sent her mother away to see about a meal for the little boy and then she spoke to her father. She said she didn't want to say anything to her mother, for fear of upsetting her since she was in the house all alone by herself, but she had had a very frightening experience.

When she had arrived home from school she had opened the door and there, crouching on the stairs, she had seen an 'extraordinary werewolf-like creature'. As she watched it had vaulted over the banister, landing with a strange 'plop' on the hallway floor, like a clawed animal might make, and then it had run or scampered away towards the rear part of the house, in the direction of the music room — and the most awful thing of all was that she couldn't stop herself running after it; she had felt impelled to follow it but when she reached the music room and found it empty, she had suddenly stopped and had become absolutely panic-stricken. But, she added, 'Don't tell mother

When the analysis of the heads had been almost completed Dr Ross had a telephone call from a journalist in the north of England who said he had met purely by chance that morning a lorry-driver who was most amused by the stories he had heard about the strange happenings associated with the stone heads because he had made them fifteen years earlier to amuse his daughter; and then for the first time Dr Ross heard the story of earlier happenings concerning the stone heads.

She learned that they had been dug up in the garden of a council house in Hexham, (a place long associated with pagan and Celtic religions) when a garden rockery was being built. They had been found four or five feet deep and they were placed on the window ledge of the house by the woman who then occupied the house and that night when she and her ten-year-old son were saying 'good night' to a younger son, about five years old, a dark creature had suddenly burst into the room, a being that she described as half-man and half-beast, a creature that battered her, knocked her little boy to the floor and then disappeared towards the front door. Now this door was closed and locked with a Yale lock, so although she knew that whatever it was would be delayed by the locked door, nevertheless, almost screaming with terror, the woman felt impelled to follow, but when she reached the front door it was standing wide open and a howling gale was coming in through the open door, although in fact it was a quiet night. That lady subsequently had a total nervous breakdown, she would not have the heads in the house another night and they were taken to a nearby museum. The local council obtained a new house for her and she left.

It was this museum that sent the heads to Dr Ross for analysis but it cannot but be interesting and puzzling to realise that until this time the scientist and her family had no idea that another family had seen an identical 'creature' in the vicinity of the strange little stone heads. When she had finished her analysis the heads were sent to a professor at the department of geology at a nearby university and it is a curious fact that these physical objects that upset one in private circumstances rarely affect things or people or have anything odd about them when they are in such a place as a museum or laboratory.

At this time Dr Ross had in her house just one rather horrible head that had constantly been in the vicinity of the stone heads for several days and nights and this really was a horrible little head —

'a real devil'. Since the stone heads had been in the house it seemed to have drawn to itself the evil from the other two heads; it had two eyes of equal size but by day its right eye would appear to be normal while its left eye was one- and-a-half times larger and at night the left eye would appear to be normal but the right eye much larger. This observation, it should be remembered, was made by a scientific academic, long used to handling such heads and working on them, day and night; heads from all over the world and from every civilization and culture.

The local vicar also felt that this particular head absorbed evil and he suggested that an experienced exorcist, whom he knew, might be able to help. So it was decided to invite the vicar and his exorcist friend, a Roman Catholic priest, to come along one evening for a glass of madeira and a chat. No mention was made of the evil heads but after an hour or so, when there was a lull in the conversation, Dr Ross mentioned that she had in her study at the moment a rather interesting head... so they casually went into the study. The visiting priest was immediately riveted by the head. He put his hand on it and said, 'This head is evil... it has been sacrificed to... it is very evil and you must get it out of your house as soon as you can... it absorbs and exudes evil.'

Next day, a Sunday, the five-year-old-son of the family came into his mother's bedroom — remember he had been told nothing of the experiences of other members of the household — and said he had just seen a funny thing: he had just been downstairs to get himself a glass of juice and on coming out of the playroom to return upstairs he had seen 'a funny black thing, half-wolf and half-man'; it had leapt upstairs ahead of him and disappeared into the spare bedroom and he had followed it — again this compulsion to follow — because he felt this awful feeling that he had to follow it, but there was nothing in the bedroom. His mother tried to comfort him by suggesting that perhaps it was just a shadow or something like that but the little boy was very sure that it was by no means so easily explained: 'Oh no, it wasn't a shadow, there was something funny about it...'

That morning after church the scientist went out into her garden and her old neighbour, a psychic person with whom Dr Ross does not have a great deal in common, went out of her way to call across, saying, out of nowhere, 'You must get rid of that head — it's evil and if you don't it will destroy you.' Dr Ross replied that she had to admit that she did not like the head and since she had finished working on it, she planned to return it next day. 'Tomorrow will be too late...' replied the neighbour; but there was little that could be done on a Sunday so preparations were made for the head to leave the house the following morning. That night at dinner Dr Ross's husband suddenly stopped eating and they all heard the characteristic 'plop' from the direction of the hallway — and he said, 'Oh, that's what you mean...

that's the sound, is it. . . very odd, certainly I've never heard anything like that before. . .' And he promised to return the head next day without fail.

During the night Dr Ross had a severe miscarriage, in fact it was almost fatal; she lost two-thirds of her blood and being allergic and unable to accept transfusions, she spent three months in bed with injections of dried blood and dried iron; these consist of the deepest possible injection and she passed out after every one... however, once the heads had gone everyone felt that the most terrible cloud had been lifted.

The stone heads were returned to the Northern museum from which they came and during the course of a lecture there the scientist met the lorry-driver who claimed to have made the heads. She said to him, 'Alright, you made the heads; well, make me another, will you?' And the head he eventually produced was nothing like the original heads, nothing like them at all; it was just the kind of thing a child might make. Remember Dr Ross is very experienced in this field and she had no doubt whatever when she first saw the heads and after careful examination that they were of pagan origin and nothing has happened to make her change her mind since. It is well known that, for each unsolved murder, half-a-dozen people claim to be responsible, although on examination it is found to have been quite impossible for them to have committed the murders, and they cannot give any information about the crimes other than that which has been published. It may be that the lorry-driver's story is on a par with this kind of confession; an attempt perhaps to achieve some kind of reflected glory in attempting to make an established or respected academic look silly.

By this time the woman in whose garden the heads had been found was still far from well and she thought the heads should be reburied in the place where they had been found; perhaps they had been placed there to protect something... this was done and the same night the woman then occupying the house, a newcomer to the area who knew nothing about the heads or the experiences that seemed to follow them, had almost identical experiences: this 'thing' coming into the house, petrifying the family, sending her into hysterics, and then she said to her husband: 'For God's sake dig those heads up...' But her sister-in-law said, 'What a lot of rubbish — all right, dig them up and I'll have them in my garden for ornaments!' This was done and she had exactly the same experience as her sister-in-law and everyone else who has had possession of the heads in their houses. There has been no satisfactory long-term analysis of the heads; the analysis of the professor of geology in no way dovetailing with that of the museum of antiquities or that of Dr Ross. The museum decided the heads were worthless and sent them back to the professor to do what he liked with them.

Dr Ross did not know that they had been returned to the professor of geology and several months passed and then one day she said to the professor: 'I keep getting letters from a doctor in London who wants to do some research and experiments with those stone heads because there is a growing feeling among archaeologists and scientists and other interested people that certain objects that have themselves been subject to intense human experience and emotions — worship, passion, sorrow, sacrifice and the rest — somehow take on vibrations which, given the right conditions, re-manifest; and it is to test this theory that the doctor wishes to borrow the stone heads, but I have made enquiries and the heads seem to have disappeared...' Then the professor told Dr Ross that he had the heads. They were sent to London where the doctor is still conducting experiments and perhaps there will be another chapter to this remarkable story one day. I have talked with Dr Ross and her husband, both at their home in Southampton and they have visited our home in Hampshire. It is one of the most curious cases that I have ever come across.

Testwood House, Totton, formerly a royal hunting lodge, a nobleman's country seat, a well-known gentleman's home, a country club and now the offices of the sherry shippers, Williams and Humbert, seems to harbour ghosts.

Heavy footsteps have been heard walking along passages covered with thick carpeting, footsteps that sounded as though they were walking on boards. Such sounds were heard by two responsible members of the staff in December 1960. The sounds seem to originate in an upstairs corridor where dogs refuse to go. One night the caretaker was making his rounds after the staff had gone home when he heard the footsteps.

A year later, in December 1961, unexplained figures were see outside the house. One autumn night the caretaker's sixteen-year-old daughter, Pauline, was returning late from a dance and had almost got to the front door of Testwood House, accompanied by her brother, when they both saw a tall man, in frock coat and tall hat, apparently trying to open the door. As they approached he vanished. Neither knew of any ghostly associations of the house. Later the same evening the same figure was seen by another witness at the back of the house.

Shortly afterwards the same figure was seen by a chef who happened to be working late in the kitchen. He became aware of someone standing silently beside him, watching, only a few feet away. Almost as soon as he became aware of the presence, it vanished. As the chef drove away from the house that night, the headlights of his car picked out the figure of a man on the drive, walking towards the front door. He noticed that the figure wore a top hat and a long overcoat with a short cape, before it suddenly disappeared. A month later another member of the staff saw a similar figure standing by one of the entrance gates in broad daylight.

A year later, in November 1962, the caretaker, Geoffrey Tebbutt, and his family were awakened by their dog barking suddenly very late one night. Thinking that there must be intruders in the grounds, the caretaker and his seventeen-year- old son, Bernard, ran across the yard to the main building where they found that the back door was rattling violently although there was no sign of anybody in the vicinity. After they had circled the building and examined all doors and windows with their torches, the caretaker's son reached the little pantry window in the oldest part of the house. Here, although the window is unglazed and protected by a metal mesh screen and vertical bars obviating the possibility of reflection, as the torchlight fell on the window the boy saw the unmistakable face of a young man staring out at him. The face, long and pale, with grey eyes, looked out unblinking and unmoving as the boy watched, petrified, until his father joined him, whereupon the face faded away. An immediate investigation revealed that the room was heavily padlocked from the outside and no one was inside the building.

Discussion with former occupants of the house produced other stories of strange happenings. The owners of the former country club spoke to me of an unexplained figure of a woman seen in one of the attic bedrooms and of a coach-and- four dashing up the drive. Local folk told of a murder committed here many years ago when a manservant killed a cook and dragged her body down the drive, across the main road and dumped it in a byway still known as Cook's Lane.

On Wednesday 20 January, 1965, a new male assistant Company Secretary, who knew nothing of the haunting, was in the entrance hall at 7.30 p.m. when he saw a man in a caped coat and tall hat sitting in a chair at the reception desk. At the same time he found that he was shivering with cold. He dashed blindly out of the front door and when he looked back the man had gone. Subsequently it transpired that the new secretary had been busy working in the 'haunted room' on the top floor and had arranged for a taxi to collect him at 7.30 p.m. He packed up his books just before this time and started to go downstairs. He was very astonished to find that the cleaners had turned all the lights out, although they knew he was working in the house, and he felt they might have left them on. He stumbled down the stairs to the first landing and then felt his way along the corridor to the other stairs and practically tripped down the first few. He said afterwards that his only thought at this time was annoyance at the darkness and the hope that the taxi would be on time and would wait. As he turned the bend in the main stairs he saw reflected in the light from the front door this figure of a man sitting at the reception desk. He had his back to the secretary and his head was tilted back, almost as though he were laughing at something. It was at that moment that the secretary felt a feeling of 'terrible cold' — he could not remember feeling so cold before — and then he was at the door and saw the lights of the taxi coming along the drive, reflected through the window.

He remembered feeling a great relief when he was outside the front door, but a further mystery presented itself when the caretaker was questioned about the lights. He said the Company Secretary was quite wrong in saying they were out, because he clearly remembered looking out of his cottage at about eight o'clock and being very annoyed that the new Company Secretary had left them all on! Both men were adamant in their respective stories on this point.

The Company Secretary drew a sketch of what he had seen and signed it; it is similar in every respect to previous descriptions of the ghost coachman and to another sketch made by someone else who saw the same ghost. The Company Secretary did not see the previous sketch before producing his own.

If there is anything in the story of a murder at Testwood House one wonders whether it could possibly account for the strange figures that have been seen at the house: the caped figure that haunts the front part of the premises; the mysterious female figure in the attic (the victim, perhaps?); the face at the pantry window (the murderer caught?); the feeling of a presence in the pantry, haunt of the cook ...

A lady who worked at Testwood House as a maid in 1911 knows nothing about any ghost coachman but says she did once hear a noise that sounded like a team of horses galloping up the drive when there was nothing to account for the sounds; she was in a room at the top of the house at the time and was told that it was the room where a former butler had murdered a cook many years before.

In 1965 The Ghost Club visited Testwood House and several members remarked on a curious 'waiting' atmosphere in the upper parts of the interesting old house where dogs frequently refuse to go up the backstairs to the 'haunted room'. We were able to establish that the back door fits tightly and does not rattle of its own accord. It seems indisputable that strange events have happened at Testwood House in the past and it seems likely that ghosts still walk there occasionally.

Was it the voice of a ghost that the occupants of the Deanery of Saint Mary's, Southampton, heard for eighteen months in 1959 and 1960?

The rector and his wife both heard a voice, independently, or could it have been the squeak of a door? Neither thought so at the time and on several occasions one or other would hear the voice and think someone was there. At first they said nothing about the matter and then they each found that the other had heard the same mysterious voice.

They said nothing to the family and when their son came home from university he, too, independently and without anyone saying anything, remarked on the mysterious voice he had heard more than once in the house... and when their daughter came home, she too heard the voice, without anyone telling her about it.

Soon the old Deanery was pulled down and only a portion was turned into a couple of flats. The mysterious voice was heard no more. The Deanery was built on the site of a monastery and those who heard the voice wondered whether it was that of a monk seeking retribution for the demolition of the monastery. It is the church of St Mary's that has been immortalized in the Bing Crosby song, The Bells of Saint Mary's. After giving a talk at South Wonston in June 1980, the wife of the rector herself told me about the mysterious voice in the Deanery.

Testwood House

UPHAM NEAR BISHOPS WALTHAM

Here, where there is an entry in the church registers that notes the cost of cleaning out the chancel after Cromwell's troops stabled their horses in the church, and where you feel that you are in the very heart of Hampshire, there is a haunted inn and a house that is gently and delightfully haunted.

Cromwell put up at the Brushmakers' Arms when he was here, preparing to attack Winchester and an alcove is pointed out as the place where the Protector made his plans. A century earlier the men who gave the inn its name frequented the area in profusion. They were the colony of brushmakers who used to congregate in the Upham area as a respite from touring the country far and wide selling their brooms that they had cut and fashioned with their own hands.

There is a story that one of these brushmakers, a man named Chickett, was a miser. He spent not a penny more than he had to and, very foolishly in those days as today, he carried all his wealth on his person, a fact that must have been known to many people. When he was at Upham he stayed at the Brushmakers' Arms, sleeping in the low-ceilinged room at the front of the inn, with his money under his pillow.

One morning his bloodstained body was found in the room but of his savings there was no sign. His murderers were never found but it is said that Chickett returns to the inn from time to time, prowling around the little room where he breathed his last... Another story says it is a local landowner who was murdered here by some enraged tenants.

Whatever or whoever haunts the room, it is something that has affected the inn dog, for on numerous occasions the animal would growl and appear very uneasy in the room, as though it saw or sensed something invisible to its human companions. I talked with a number of local people who had lived in the vicinity all their lives and several of them said maybe the room was haunted and maybe it wasn't — but they wouldn't spend a night there anyway.

The haunted house is semi-detached and not all that old, but the occupants, who welcomed me there in August 1980, have many times encountered a very powerful and pleasant perfume which they have never been able to explain. They have woken up in the middle of the night with the perfume filling the bedroom; they have encountered it in the middle of winter, downstairs. Suddenly they are aware of the overwhelming and delightful smell and, just as suddenly, it is gone. Fancy, you may say, pure imagination... then how do you explain the incident when a neighbour asked about the brand of washing powder that the householder used... this neighbour said she had often noticed a beautiful scent when she passed the house, it seemed to begin at one end of the house and finish at the other, outside the adjoining house it had completely gone. She thought it must be a special washing powder although she could not see any washing. Needless to say, the occupant had not done any washing and she only uses ordinary washing powder anyway, not perfumed. But she knew what the neighbour had been talking about, she and her husband had smelt it many times and they hope they will encounter it many more times in the future. A psychic scent perhaps, some whiff of a long-forgotten incident that has in some way become attached to the house; or is it explicable in mundane terms? You take your choice.

SOUTHSEA

The house in Saint Michael's Road that was once a workhouse, then offices administering Corporation welfare, and then such services as marriage guidance counselling, has long been reputed to be haunted.

The inexplicable figure of an old man, wearing a top hat, a long grey coat and carrying an old carved stick, is said to have been seen in the vicinity of Number 1 for many years. The tapping of his stick is also heard as well as his dragging footsteps.

In 1971 there were numerous reports from different members of the staff at that time; some said they had seen the figure, some said they had heard him and some said they had both seen and heard the old man who always seems to appear in places where it would be impossible for a visitor to be and by the time the person seeing the figure begins to wonder who the man is and what he is doing, the figure has disappeared. There are grounds for believing that the figure is that of the original beadle who used to be in charge of the building a century and a half ago. Certainly, descriptions compared.

VENTNOR, ISLE OF WIGHT

A ghostly event, if not a ghostly appearance, took place at Craigie Lodge, a residence near Ventnor, in October 1921, and received considerable publicity.

The property was at one time occupied by John Oliver Hobbes, the pseudonym of Mrs Pearl Mary Theresa Craigie, hence the name of the house. A lane divided the property and on the side of the lane farthest from the house was a grassy terrace, overlooking a tennis court. The gardener of the then tenant of Craigie Lodge was planting shrubs in this terrace when he unearthed the lower jawbone of a child. He took it to his mistress, Mrs Capell, who happened to have staying with her Mrs Hugh Pollock, a psychometrist. Years later I talked with her about the incident.

Further digging unearthed the entire skeleton of a child and Mrs Pollock took a bone and placed it against her forehead. After a moment she declared that another skeleton was lying close to where the child's remains had been found. A second skeleton was duly discovered, that of a woman. The ensuing arguments and legal wrangling have no place here but it is clear that it was no coincidence that the second skeleton was found. The Craigie Lodge incident brought to the fore, perhaps for the first time, the fascinating puzzle of clairvoyance and psychometry.

WATERLOOVILLE

'Hopfield'

It is to Mrs Sheila White of Saint Helens, the lady who experienced the 'Night of the Lights' (see Ashey Down), that I am indebted for details of the remarkable haunting associated with a house called 'Hopfield' because, at the time it was built, early in the nineteenth century, the area was largely composed of fields put down to hops.

The house was built by Edward Fawkes for his family and descendants, with the expressed intention that it should remain in the possession of the family for always. However, it was not to be, and when Helen McFarlane, great-granddaughter of Edward Fawkes, was ten years old the family decided to move to Southsea and 'Hopfield' was let on a three-year agreement to an elderly retired naval officer and his wife, a childless couple who were both ardent students of psychic matters.

For a time all was well and then the naval officer telephoned to say the 'spirit' of Edward Fawkes had appeared in the house to both him and his wife, intimating that they had no right to be living there and threatening them with violence unless they moved out at once. There would be no peace for anyone in the house, they were given to understand, who was not a Fawkes.

At first Helen Me Farlane's father did not take the matter very seriously but soon he received a letter from a naval officer asking for permission to sublet for the remaining period of the lease as it was quite impossible for him and his wife to remain there, because of the repeated appearances of Edward Fawkes and his continuing threats.

The sub-letting was agreed to and 'Hopfield' was let to a middle-aged widow and her daughter. Both were in good health when they moved in but suddenly one morning the mother was found dead in bed and the daughter begged to be allowed to give up the sub-lease. She was allowed to do so and quickly moved out.

By this time the family were beginning to become very worried about the whole matter and they decided to sell the house rather than let it, as they did not want to return there. The new owner was a military captain and his wife, recently retired from the Army after many years of service abroad.

Early one morning the butler discovered the body of Captain Playfair with one of his own Indian daggers in his back in the hall of 'Hop- field'. The murder was never solved and the widow moved out as soon as possible.

Once more the house was sold and this time it passed into the hands of the Nowell family. By now it was the 1920s and the wealthy new owners soon altered and transformed the somewhat gaunt and sinister house into a beautiful home. The Nowells and Sheila White's family were great friends; Sheila and the Nowell children, a son and a daughter, were contemporary in age and it was at this period that Sheila first visited the house she came to know so well.

Not that she ever fell in love with the building. She visited 'Hopfield' with her family and the Nowells before they bought the property and to this day she can recall the feeling of evil that pervaded the rambling, cold and dark house; one stairway area she found particularly disconcerting. But the two families usually spent the Christmas holiday period together and after 'Hopfield' had been enlarged, renovated and utterly changed, that first Christmas was spent at 'Hopfield', with her pet dog Scraggie.

She awoke to the unusual sound of Scraggie growling. She reached out for the bedside lamp but in the unfamiliar room could not find it. She sat up — and received a crack on the head that felt as though an iron bar had struck her. She dropped back on the bed and then slowly sat up again — the same thing happened and then she began to experience a feeling of panic. For one thing Scraggie's growling was louder and fiercer but the odd thing was that although she knew she was in bed she felt as though she was enclosed in some sort of cage and that seemed to be what she cracked her head on whenever she tried to sit up... she felt all around her carefully and came to the conclusion that she was now lying underneath the bed instead of on top of it. Slowly she edged her way out, found the lamp and brought light to the dark room.

Scraggie was still terrified. He was crouched in his basket, his eyes fixed on the bedroom door, his hackles raised and growling quietly. Following the direction in which he was looking Sheila saw the door handle turn and the door slowly open. No one was there and no one came in but Sheila had had enough. She snatched up her dressing-gown, picked up the dog and ran into her parents' room, almost in tears. The time was just after 1 a.m.

For the rest of that stay at 'Hopfield', Sheila's father occupied the bedroom that had been allocated to her and she slept with her mother. Her father also found that the bedroom door opened by itself; in fact, he became tired of closing it, time after time, night after night, and eventually he left it open. He had no other experience in the room and they did not mention the matter to the Nowells. On subsequent visits both Sheila and her father heard noises at night that disturbed them, puzzled them and occasionally frightened them but again they did not mention the matter to their hosts.

Perhaps it would have been better had the Nowells been warned of the atmosphere and feeling in the house that was experienced by some people but all too soon tragedy overcame the family that had bought 'Hopfield' and had decided to alter it and live in it...

The Nowells had a son, a pleasant and clever young man who was on vacation from Oxford. He seemed to have no troubles or worries and indeed a brilliant future seemed to be ahead for him. One morning he went down into the basement of the haunted house and almost blew his head off with a shotgun. His mother was shattered and died herself very soon afterwards. Within months Mr Nowell collapsed in his dressing room. He was dead when he was found. Now only the Nowell daughter remained. She fled and the place was boarded up and left empty. It became overgrown, began to deteriorate and was shunned by the local people. Eventually it was sold and then sold again. Today it has become a series of flats, amid the maze of dwellings that is modern Waterlooville. One wonders whether strange incidents still occur within those cold walls that have seen so much tragedy and unhappiness;

whether the occupants are aware of the stories associated with the house they live in or whether the hauntings have at last run their course.

WHERWELL NEAR ANDOVER

Here there is macabre legend and a haunted priory.

The very strange story of the Cockatrice of Wherwell concerns the cockatrice-shaped vane on the tower of Wherwell Church and the tradition that a nunnery once flourished in this delightful village. It is said that a duck that was kept by the nuns once laid an egg that hatched into a cockatrice (a fabulous reptile with a death-dealing glare!) which grew and grew until it became an enormous monster. The nuns continued to feed it, having secured it in a specially-constructed den; but no one dared to approach too close. Apparently it escaped and after killing some of the nuns, sought shelter in some nearby woods. The nuns sought the aid of a woodman named Green who tracked the beast but found the task of killing it more than he had bargained for. At length he adopted a subtle plan. He polished up a metal shield until it shone like a mirror and placing it where the monster cockatrice would find it, he hid nearby and waited.

As he had foreseen, the great beast, seeing itself seemingly faced by an equally fearsome monster, proceeded to the attack and while it was so engaged, the resourceful woodman slew the animal.

To this day the place is known as Green's Copse and a representation of the Cockatrice of Wherwell is preserved by the County Museum Service.

Close to the church, with its thirteenth century sculpture and sleeping figure of a nun who was prioress here in the fourteenth century, there are remains of a seventeenth century stone wall that was once part of the priory destroyed by Henry VIII. The priory was founded in Saxon times by Queen Elfreida in remorse for having her stepson murdered at Corfe Castle, so that her own son could become king. She retired from the world to Wherwell and, in an effort to atone for what she had done, 'clothed her pampered body in haircloth, slept at night upon the ground without a pillow, mortified her flesh with every kind of penance' and founded a priory. One wonders whether it is her ghost and that of her followers who are seen from time to time, a phantom pair of nuns carrying candles. They have been seen only at dusk in the late autumn and they apparently frequent the churchyard and fragmentary ruins of their lost priory.

WINCHESTER

This fine, historic city, capital of England before London, has some fine old houses and hospitals, together with an ancient cross, a castle and its gateway housing a small museum, numerous quaint passages and crooked lanes, a lovely old cloister, a great school, a medieval church and a cathedral where Izaak Walton and Jane Austen lie buried. Here were crowned William the Conqueror and Richard I and here, too, Queen Mary was married to Philip of Spain; in the great thirteenth century hall, all that remains of Winchester Castle, is to be seen King Arthur's Round Table, an interesting relic that probably dates from Tudor times since a Tudor rose decorates the centre. St Swithun is said to have expressed a wish to be buried outside the church he knew — in his humility he wished for the foot of the passer-by and the rain and sun from the heavens to fall upon his grave, and there his body lay for more than a century. A chapel was eventually erected over the site of the grave in the north-east corner of the church and faint traces of the building can still be found. The skull of St Swithun is said to have been removed to Canterbury in the eleventh century and the arm of this patron saint of Winchester was a much treasured possession at Peterborough. The cathedral itself is haunted. A phantom monk has been seen walking along the aisle and mounting invisible steps and phantom figures have been photographed within the precincts of the cathedral.

Indeed Winchester has a variety of ghosts and to start with we will look at two haunted inns and a poltergeist haunting that has some unusual features.

The Eclipse Inn, scene of the last hours of Dame Alicia Lisle, who also haunts Moynes Court (see Ringwood) has long been reputed to appear in ghostly form in one of the upstairs passages of this ancient hostelry that squats in the shadow of the cathedral. It was on 2 September, 1685, that Dame Alicia was beheaded there. She had given refuge to two survivors of Monmouth's rebellion. She faced a charge of treason before Judge Jeffreys and listened with calm dignity to the ranting and raving and the awful sentence that was eventually reduced to execution.

A scaffold was built against the timbered front of the old inn and Dame Alicia spent her last night in an upper room at the Eclipse and it is that area of the establishment that has been haunted ever since by a tall, motionless figure in grey; sometimes she is seen in the bedroom itself but more often in the passageway outside. She has been seen by servants and visitors and one maid has related her experience: 'I was cleaning the carpet on the first floor landing at about ten o'clock in the morning when I had a feeling that someone was watching me. I looked over my shoulder and saw a tall woman in a long grey woollen dress standing in a corner of the landing. I could not see her face, just the figure. It was an odd experience which left me rather shaken. I saw the figure a second time about eleven one morning when, in the same passageway, I felt someone brush against me, giving me a gentle push. I called out but nobody was there and then I saw the grey form I had seen before, in the same place. Although it was all very uncanny I can't say that I really felt frightened.'

In September, 1980, I talked with a former licensee of the Eclipse who told me that she had no doubt whatsoever that the place was haunted. While she was there visitors, staff and personal friends, who knew nothing of the reputed appearance of the lady in grey, including some American visitors, told her they had seen a grey lady in the passageway and noticed strange noises in the haunted room. One couple said they were awakened at dead of night by the sound of rough voices outside and the sound of hammering as though something made of wood was being hastily built. When they looked out the sounds immediately stopped and the road outside was completely deserted.

The Eclipse Inn

Old as the Eclipse may be, the Hyde Tavern in Hyde Street may be older still. It was certainly haunted when David Rice and his wife were there in the 1960s and may still be haunted today. It was by no means unusual for the Rices to find themselves wide awake in the early hours to see and feel the blankets and bedclothes slowly slipping from the bed: 'pulled' they used to say. At other times they would wake to see all the bedclothes already removed from the bed and piled up in a heap several feet away from the bed.

Beds and bedclothes do seem to have an overwhelming attraction for many ghosts and 'unseen guests' in Hampshire as elsewhere. At the Hyde Tavern this particular disturbance was reported many times not only by the landlord and his wife but also by friends and visitors who were not told what might happen. According to some accounts the ghost responsible is that of a woman who, centuries ago, sought shelter here when the premises were used by pilgrims but, for some unknown reason, she was refused warmth and shelter and died here, cold and hungry.

There is also a very old house, near the cathedral, where one wall is said to be that of William the Conqueror's Old Palace. Many strange and unexplained sounds have been heard in the house and some years ago a friend told me that she stayed one night in the house. The owner was quite used to the odd noises that seemed to emanate from the wall and she would say, 'Oh, that's only William again...' but her little Pomeranian dog would cower and tremble in terror, its eyes following something invisible to its human companions, along the wall and sometimes round the room. During the course of her night in an old panelled room, my friend suddenly found herself wide awake and she heard what sounded like a hand fumbling along the panelling. It seemed to go all round the room, skirting doors and cupboards. She lay there, too frightened to move, until daylight and was thankful she was spending only one night in the house.

For more than ten years 'something' has been haunting Joyce Bowles and her family in their council house at 45 Quarry Road. I went to see Mrs Bowles twice and found her to be a good witness, quiet, ready to help and fully cooperative in my attempts to understand her truly remarkable story.

Objects flew across the room, I was told, knocks sounded on doors, heavy furniture lurched across a bedroom without human aid, electric light switches turned themselves on and off, the sound of heavy footsteps vibrated through the house and there were physical presences: an elderly man, a lady in white and a nun.

Before we look at Joyce Bowles's extraordinary story, consider for a moment the evidence of other people: neighbours have seen the face of a strange woman at the window of number 45, seemingly beckoning to passers-by — at times when the house is empty of human inhabitants; several friends of the Bowles have seen the ghost of a man in the house (he is known as 'the man in black' because he always wears a long black cloak fastened at the neck with a chain and two brass buttons). Next door neighbour Mrs Bessie Shears was in the house one morning talking to Joyce Bowles when suddenly she found that she could not move her feet, she was rooted to the spot; she saw nothing but at the same time Joyce Bowles saw the man in black standing behind her friend. Then the ghost moved and Mrs Shear's legs returned to normal. Another friend witnessed the movement of furniture in the bedroom and heard strange sounds and noises, saw a mattress move by itself and heard the sound of footsteps. A milkman saw a chair move. The Revd Ramsdale Whalley, official exorcist to the diocese of Winchester, said he could 'sense' something in one of the bedrooms; his divining-rod dipped and he conducted two services of exorcism but they had little effect. Mrs Ann Strickland saw candlesticks fly across a room and felt her hair stroked when she was (apparently) alone in the room. Mrs Renee Pratt and her husband Tom saw books remove themselves from a bookcase. Mrs Shears saw the lady in white and felt a touch when no one was with her...

Mr and Mrs Bowles and their four sons, who have never had any special interest in ghosts and hauntings, were delighted when they had the opportunity of moving into the three-bedroomed semi-detached house in 1968 but it was not long before odd things happened. Joyce Bowles began to hear her name called: 'Joyce... Joyce... Joyce...' and she would go from room to room trying to find where the voice came from. Then one night, when her husband was on night shift for British Rail at Winchester Station, Joyce Bowles suddenly found herself wide awake. 'Some noise had disturbed me and now I could hear it clearly — the sound of footsteps walking around the bed towards me. I felt a pressure on my chest, making me struggle for breath. At the same time I felt myself being lifted bodily several inches above the bed... a church clock struck midnight and the street lights went out, leaving the room in total darkness. I was absolutely terrified. I hid under the bedclothes and heard the clock strike one, two, three and four o'clock before I could pluck up the courage to go downstairs and make myself a cup of tea.'

Subsequently the disturbances ran practically the whole gamut of strange happening reported from haunted houses. Strange smells, especially an old, musty smell and a smell like rotten eggs often seemed to precede appearances of the man in black. There were touchings, movements of objects, noises, sensations of coldness, voices, inexplicable visions...

Mrs Joyce Bowles pointed out to me the place where once she had seen the figure of a nun. She had just left a friend in the lounge and went to go upstairs to fetch something. As she was about to put her foot on the bottom step she saw someone standing on the landing. It looked like a nun. The figure appeared to be absolutely normal. 'She wore a long habit complete with headdress and had a pleasant face; she appeared to be quite young.' The figure was looking steadily down the stairs towards Mrs Bowles, who was too surprised to move or speak. One arm of the solid-looking nun was raised and seemed to pointing towards the landing window. The next moment the figure had completely disappeared.

By the autumn of 1973 things had become so bad that Joyce Bowles was beginning to think that she was mentally ill. But her doctor assured her that there was nothing wrong and anyway other people heard and saw things as well as her and her family.

A friend who was interested in the subject of haunted houses came to stay for a week and brought a Bible and some garlic. She shared a bedroom with Joyce and in the middle of the night the room suddenly went ice cold, they heard scratching noises, then a loud bang like a gunshot, some of the bedroom furniture moved by itself as they watched. The mattress seemed alive and lifted and moved of its own accord 'as if a huge hand was there...'The two women were levitated for about thirty seconds but eventually, as always, things became quiet and although Joyce Bowles told me she had certainly been frightened many times and so had her family and friends and visitors, yet she is convinced that there is nothing evil in the house.

One of my visits to Mrs Bowles came soon after her milkman had had the scare of his life. He had been enjoying a morning cup of coffee when suddenly she had seen him put down his cup and run out of the house. She went after him and he told her he had seen one of the armchairs lift itself off the floor, tilt over backwards and then slide along the living-room wall. He was one of the people who used to scoff at experiences related by Mrs Bowles, but not. any more! I sat in the chair that moved by itself. It is a heavy, comfortable chair and I could find no plausible reason how it could possibly rise off the floor by itself, tilt or slide across the floor.

One night Joyce Bowles again found herself awake in the middle of the night. She was alone in bed at the time but she distinctly heard her name called. She sat up in bed and saw a 'brilliant cross of light that hung in the sky, shimmering...'

Radio and television reporters have found that their equipment has been mysteriously affected by 'something'; one reporter slumped into a sort of trance in the 'haunted' chair and while he was unconscious two candlesticks flew across the room and a musty smell pervaded that part of the room. When he recovered consciousness he said he had had a kind of vision in which a group of robed people were singing. He didn't stay long after that experience.

The forces of energy or power that produce the strange happenings may emanate in some way that we do not yet understand from Joyce Bowles herself. She is usually present when anything happens and events seem to centre around her. It is a strange case and I came away anxious to conduct a lengthy series of experiments in the house and involving the participation of Joyce Bowles but it is not easy to arrange things to the convenience of all concerned and then things became rather quieter and we did not want to do anything that might reverse this development.

Photographs of ghosts are sometimes sent to me and while they are always interesting I think that they often have a natural explanation. For example it is said that some modern cameras that take 35mm film are fitted with a device that makes double exposure impossible since you cannot release the shutter, having taken one exposure, until you have wound on the film; but most things can happen very occasionally and of course it is the occasional event that is remembered. I have before me as I write a double exposure, taken with such a camera, that I took myself by accident. Obviously something went wrong, but it is the camera that has produced a very odd image, there is nothing wrong with the object being photographed... nevertheless there have been some very strange photographic results obtained under seemingly stringent conditions and circumstances and one is a photograph shown to me by Alasdair Alpin MacGregor and taken in Winchester Cathedral.

The photographer, Thomas L. Taylor, is an electrical engineer living near Wolverhampton and he took the photograph in 1957. It received wide publicity and then a Winchester cleric sought to explain the photograph in rational terms in the columns of the Daily Telegraph. But perhaps it is not as easily explained as might be expected.

Mr Taylor was on holiday with his wife and daughter and between 10 and 11 o'clock on 19 August, 1957, while in Winchester Cathedral, he took two photographs using Kodachrome film, from a central position, of the High Altar and the carved stone screen. This part of the cathedral was quite deserted at the time.

When the colour transparencies were developed

and returned to him he found that the earlier exposure reproduced the scene exactly as he had seen it and devoid of any human being but the second exposure, taken under precisely the same conditions, showed what appeared to be a number of human male figures in medieval costume.

Certain Winchester clergy, as I have said, sought to explain the thirteen figures in terms of reflection or a freak combination of light and shade but photographic experts, examining the transparency in magnification, were satisfied that the figures bore no resemblance to the sculptured figures that the clergy thought must have been reflected in some odd way and, if the figures on the transparency were reflections of the recumbent sculptured figures, how was it that these figures appeared upright in the photographic representation? It is certainly one of the more interesting 'psychic photographs' that have come to my attention and I would be interested to hear of any other apparently inexplicable figures that have appeared on photographs taken in Winchester Cathedral.

At one time Prebendary House was apparently haunted by a frightening apparition. Lady Chatterton, daughter of the Revd Lascelles Iremonger, prebendary of Winchester cathedral and vicar of Goodworth Clatford near Andover, before the First World War, has left a record of her experience.

Her mother had been rather ill at the time but was then convalescent and Lady Chatterton left her in the drawing-room in excellent spirits and retired to bed. Suddenly finding herself wide awake in the middle of the night, Lady Chatterton saw the figure of a woman she took to be her mother, dreadfully pale, lying on her bed with blood flowing from her lips. She tried to touch the figure and found that she could not do so... throwing on a cloak she rushed to her mother's room and found her just as she had seen the figure in her own bedroom, with the sheet covered in blood and two doctors in attendance.

Her mother was delighted to see her, although too ill to speak, and pressed her hand. One of the doctors told her that the danger was now past and she had not been sent for as her mother had not wished her to be disturbed. The story is a typical example of a ghost of the living; phantom appearances that are probably much more numerous than we suspect.

Dr William Lyon Phelps was a teacher of English Literature at Yale University. In his Autobiography he tells of a visit that he and his wife made to Winchester and to the house where Jane Austen lived.

'We had a curious experience in front of this house. It was a cloudless morning. I asked my wife to take a picture in front of the house; accordingly the camera was pointed at the front door. This door was closed and there was no one in front of it or near it. The camera clicked. But when the picture was developed there was a woman in black standing close to the door. We have no explanation whatever for this, so we have decided to call the unknown the ghost of Jane Austen. It was such a clear day that every corner of the porch and of the front door appeared in sharp relief; we could almost have seen a fly. There was absolutely nothing; but there stands the woman in the picture.'

Hyde Tavern

WRITERS' MONTHLY INTERVIEW, JANUARY 1997

Alan Williams is the author of *The Blackheath Seance Parlour* (2013), a mixture of gothic horror and historical fiction, with an additional injection of humour. He conducted an interview with Underwood in 1997, which appeared in a publication he was editor of at the time - *Writers' Monthly*.

[Alan Williams]: *Peter Underwood is one of the world's most renowned parapsychologists and prolific authors on the subject of ghosts and the supernatural. Born in Letchworth Garden City in Hertfordshire in 1923, his first awareness of the possibility of a spirit world occurred the evening after his father died at the age of none. Underwood saw his father's spirit move through the house and awoke his mother, who also saw him.*

Thus began Underwood's fascination with parapsychology and led him to investigate hauntings with friends. Over the years, the investigations became more frequent, and employed more sophisticated means of detection. His quest was to rule out all natural explanations before seriously considering other phenomenon. Over the years he has exposed some of the allegedly more haunted spots to be nothing more than natural phenomenon or fraud and brought to the eye of critics, some un-

fathomable evidence [...]

> [Peter Underwood]: "I was only a child when I saw my father's spirit but certainly, even in those early days, it opened my eyes to the possibility that there was something else. When I started investigating seriously, I don't think I was trying to prove the existence of spirits to anyone else, I was more intrigued by it, and was looking to find answers for myself.
>
> "New cases come to me mainly through letters. I get a tremendous amount of mail. People write and invite me to come to their homes because they suspect something unusual or claim to be haunted. But generally nine tenths of those are subjective, but some are very interesting."

As doctor's get swamped at social occasions with people's ailments, Underwood is also besieged with people's grizzly tales.

> "I try to keep a low profile when I'm out because otherwise people tend to come up and tell you their stories wherever you go. When people realise that you have an interest in ghosts, they come up to you and start a conversation by saying 'Ghosts? You don't believe in ghosts do you?' And then I say, 'Well you know, until you've experienced it, you really don't know. And the more I

study it, the more I think it is real'. Then they say 'Really. Well I...,' and launch into telling you about their own experiences.

"You really can't blame people for thinking you're a bit nuts if they haven't experienced something themselves. You can't prove it to them because when it comes down to it, personal experience is the only one that counts. People ask me to prove it to them but I wouldn't dream of it. What I do say, if they are sufficiently interested, is to look at the evidence. There is so much."

In A Guide to Ghosts and Haunted Places (1996), *Underwood recounts visiting a home where phantom music is played. During his visit, he hears the music and becomes suspicious. He searches the room for speakers and eventually sits on the arm chair that the occupier has left to make tea. There, beneath the heavily padded arms, he discovers buttons that trigger the music in other rooms. "Ah! You've found my little secret, have you?' said the owner returning to the room, "...Anyway, it will all be removed by tomorrow and there won't be proof of anything..."*

"I don't get angry with people who set up hauntings as a hoax, but it's quite rare that I will fall for them. When I first meet someone we have a very in-depth chat and very often, you can tell within ten minutes if a case isn't real. And then you say that it was a pleasure meeting them but you do have a rather busy day and leave. If they personally are getting some fun out of it, that's no problem."

Another example was when Underwood was asked to investigate a poltergeist haunting in a family home. The focus of the haunting seemed to surround the young teenage daughter and a potted plant that kept moving around the house.

Suspicious, Underwood drilled a small hole in the plant pot and filled it with fine sand. He also smeared doors with substances that would dye hands purple on contact. In particular, he paid attention to bedroom doors, which were locked from the outside, and the plant pot.

The following morning the plant had been moved, and a trail of sand showed its path. However, the bedroom doors remained untouched. But on inspection, the daughter's feet and hands showed traces of sand and the purple dye. She had been climbing out of her window each night and letting herself in through the front door.

"Undoubtedly a lot of hauntings are purely for publicity purposes. Though I remember a time when if a pub or castle was haunted no one would go there. Today of course, people go to them in crowds.

"I have to admit that I rarely get nervous about spending nights at houses that are haunted. I don't just sit and wait, usually I'm with a number of people and there are machines that need to be set up and monitored. So I'm pretty busy all through the night. I've jumped through hearing noises a few times but more often than not, you witness nothing. Even when you do, your main concern is getting it recorded, so you are more concerned with the machinery than actually watching the event yourself. And a lot of times, of course, it does not register on film, which is another great disappointment.

"We do have video film and we do have recordings of strange phenomena but it really doesn't mean anything to people if they were not there to witness it in person. People will hear footsteps and think - so what, but because I was there, I knew no one was in that corridor."

The technology that accompanies an investigation is far from unsophisticated and varies depending on the type of haunting reported. A typical haunting will require the following; cameras with slow, regular, fast and infra-red films, another camera for time exposure facilities, a Polaroid camera, notebooks, graph paper, pens of various colours, sound recording apparatus, including normal, miniature and very sensitive, extending leads, thermometers (again regular, maximum/minimum and thermographs [an instrument that produces a trace or image representing a record of the varying temperature or infrared radiation over an area or during a period of time]), torches, batteries and spare bulbs, measuring tapes, black cotton, colour adhesive tape, gummed and self adhesive (to seal rooms, doorways and windows), tie-on luggage labels, mirrors, candles, matches, screws, nails, panel pins, a hammer, luminous paint, a strain gauge (to measure the force necessary to close or open doors and windows), a spring balance (to measure the weight of obstacles that are moved by paranormal means) and containers to collect suspicious material. This is just for a standard haunting.

"There are various audio-tapes that claim to be proof of hauntings but the trouble with tapes is that everything on them can be discredited. I remember once listening to a tape recording made by someone else inside Borley Church and all of those sounds could be replicated by closing doors or walking or moving objects.

"One of the most common phenomena is that ghosts do make a room or certain parts of a room cold. This always registers on thermometers. The reason for this is down to the shifts in energy."

Cold spots appear to be a constant in the changing world of psychic phenomenon, but over the ages, mediums have allegedly produced ectoplasm, project voices and even conjured spirits into rooms. But these fashions in mediumship, tended to change when electricity, lights and video cameras were introduced.

"I have been in a room where a medium has allegedly produced ectoplasm. The medium was tied to a chair in the middle of the rather dimly lit room and globules of the substance began to pour from his mouth, reaching down to his lap. People claimed to see faces in it etc. But, you know, the ectoplasm has disappeared back into the body by the time the lights are switched on and no one is allowed to go close, so you never get to examine it or get a closer look.

"I have also been present at around six exorcisms and to be quite honest, I don't see how the idea behind exorcism makes it work. Exorcism is the power of a force of good, over a force of evil. Well I've never felt that there is anything evil about ghosts.

"What I have found in the cases of exorcisms that I have been involved in, is that the individuals become effected and not the ghost. They tend to believe the ghost has gone because the house has been exorcised. Rarely have we ever actually noticed the disappearance of the ghost. The people in the house who still see and hear the phenomenon try to find other explanations, appeasing themselves by saying, 'Well it can't be a ghost because the house has been exorcised'. But the events go on and on until they realise that it actually never went away at all, and that things are exactly the same. I can't deny that some exorcisms have had a positive effect, but generally they tend to support the individuals emotionally.

"People can often see ghosts because they have an intense emotional need to see them. If they have lost someone then they are already halfway there. They already have a strong link. Undoubtedly the support of the church does help a great number of people when they have lost someone and are emotional, but I'm not sure if it's necessary to bring in an exorcist.

"Even though I have visited hundreds of places and regions to compile my books, I still find it enormously enjoyable. The research and the investigation side to writing a book is the fun part - the actual writing is the hard part, but I still thoroughly enjoy writing them. It's also interesting meeting people who read my work. And now, of course, I'm getting to the age where I'm getting letters from people who say that they have been interested in my books all their lives and remember reading them as children.

"Aside from my work on psychic research, I've also written some biographies. I wrote the Boris Karloff biography* which went down so well that the publisher said 'We must do another showbiz personality' and we thought and thought and he rang me up one night and said I've got the man - Danny la Rue. And I thought 'Oh no', but he was enthusiastic and it went from there. It wasn't a very happy experience. Danny didn't want it done at all. He was about to write his own at the time, so I think he thought it was a big unnecessary. He's done one since. But that's an experience I don't want to repeat."

If you are interested in ghosts and other psychic phenomena, Underwood's books are well worth reading. He treats the subject with the intelligent and impartial observation that many books by his contemporaries lack.

WROXALL NEAR VENTNOR, ISLE OF WIGHT

Nearby Appuldurcombe House was once used as a refuge for Benedictine monks expelled from their home abbey at Solesmes in France. Later it was the seat of the mighty Worseley family whose connections with the district include the nearby Sir Richard Worseley Inn. But it is with one of the sad and disturbed monks that the tiny hamlet of Redhill Lane has long been associated.

It is said that this monk was mad and his brothers, anxious to avoid any possible scandal, locked him up deep inside the great house all day and only let him out at night when he would thankfully emerge into the clean night air and wander happily and harmlessly through the fields and along the pathways and over the farmsteads. His brothers had armed him with a handbell to that his presence would not alarm anyone and the slow, mournful ring would echo through the surrounding countryside as the monk, happy in his madness, wandered aimlessly here and there. The local people became accustomed to the ringing bell, gently breaking the silence of the night, and by and large they endured the small inconvenience with pity for the poor monk. But, when he died a few years after he came to Appuldurcombe, there was no relief or respite for the local people for the well-known ringing of the mad monk of Appuldurcombe continued without interruption.

On fine, moonlit nights, the kind of nights when the poor bemused monk would be let out, and when he would most enjoy his impulsive nocturnal wanderings; on such nights, even to this day, there are those who say they sometimes hear the ring of a ghostly handbell or catch a glimpse of a meandering grey monk-like figure wandering the countryside and occasionally skipping in joy across the fields and about the lanes near Appuldurcombe.

ACKNOWLEDGEMENTS

The author gratefully acknowledges the generous help and co-operation that he has received from the Hampshire County Museum Service, Bramshill Police College, City Archivists and Librarians, and in particular: Hope Alexander, R. Andrews, Dennis Bardens, Joyce Bowles, Gerald Coke, Barbara Cross, Count Slade de Pomeroy, Betty Doxford, Ralph Dutton, T. Ewens, Midge Gifford, Ann Gordon, Mr and Mrs Gregory, Dr Peter Hilton-Rowe, Mary and Peter Holmes, Sir Westrow Hulse, Air Commodore R. C. Jonas, Michael Joy, J. M. Knowles, G. Latham, Kenneth Lee, Helen McFarlane, Lord Montague of Beaulieu, Diana Norman, Margaret Royal, Dorothea St Hill Bourne, Paul Sangster, Michael Sedgwick, Dick Sheppard, L. N. Welch, Marguerite White, Shiela White, H. Widnell, and Virginia Wilkinson. On a personal note he is grateful for the help and interest of his wife Joyce Elizabeth and for the companionship of his grandson Toby on some of his visits to Hampshire's haunted houses.

ABOUT THE AUTHOR

Peter Underwood

Peter Underwood was President of the Ghost Club (founded 1862) from 1960-1993 and probably heard more first-hand ghost stories than any man alive. He was a long-standing member of The Society of Psychical Research, Vice-President of the Unitarian Society for Psychical Studies, a member of The Folklore Society, The Dracula Society and the Research Committee of the Psychic Research Organization, he wrote extensively, and was a seasoned lecturer and broadcaster. He took part in the first official investigation into a haunting; sat with physical and mental mediums and conducted investigations at seances. He was present at exorcisms, experiments at dowsing, precognition, clairvoyance, hypnotism, regression; he conducted world-wide tests in telepathy and extra-sensory perception, and personally investigated scores of haunted houses across the country. He possessed comprehensive files of alleged hauntings in every county of the British Isles and many foreign countries, and his knowledge and experience resulted in his being consulted on psychic and occult matters by the BBC and ITV. His many books include the first two comprehensive gazetteers of ghosts and hauntings in England, Scotland and Ireland and two books that deal with twenty different occult subjects. Highlights from his published work include 'Nights in Haunted Houses' (1993), which collects together the results of group investigations, 'The Ghosts of Borley' (1973), his classic account of the history of 'the most haunted house in England', 'Hauntings' (1977), which re-examines ten classic cases of haunting in the light of modern knowledge, 'No Common Task' (1983), which reflects back upon his life as a 'ghost hunter', and 'The Ghost Hunter's Guide' (1986), which gives the reader all the advice necessary to become one. Born at Letchworth Garden City in Hertfordshire, he lived for many years in a small village in Hampshire.

BOOKS BY THIS AUTHOR

Ghosts Of North West England

The ghostly little monk of Foulridge and the giant apparition from Heaton Norris are just two of the denizens of the North-West you might not care to meet on a dark, stormy evening. But for those intrepid souls whose hearts quicken at the thought of eerie footsteps and muffled groans Peter Underwood has assembled an impressive collection of traditional legends.

Ghosts Of Kent

The first expert exploration of the haunted houses and authentic ghosts of Kent by the [former] President of the Ghost Club, Peter Underwood.

Karloff: The Life Of Boris Karloff

Boris Karloff was the most famous of all horror

actors. His memorable portrayal of the Frankenstein monster added a new word to English dictionaries.

Hauntings: New Light On The Greatest True Ghost Stories Of The World

In this fascinating account of the best-attested cases of haunting - Hampton Court, the demon drummer of Bedworth, the Wesley ghost, Glamis, Borley Rectory and many others - Britain's foremost ghost-hunter has brought to light a wealth of valuable new evidence. Using the results of many years of research and personal investigation, and providing detailed plans and original photographs, new theories are put forward to change our ideas about these hauntings.

This Haunted Isle

Peter Underwood has personally visited the historic buildings and sites of Britain, and here presents a wealth of intriguing legends and new stories of ghostly encounters from more than a hundred such throughout the United Kingdom.
From Abbey House in Cambridge to Zennor in Cornwall, this is an A to Z of the haunted houses of Britain. At Bramshill in Hampshire — now a police training college — there have been so many sightings that even sceptical police officers have had to admit that the place is haunted. Beautiful Leeds

Castle in Kent has a large, phantom black dog; there is an Elizabethan gentleman (seen by a Canon of the Church of England!) at Croft Castle; a Pink Lady at Coughton Court; a prancing ghost jester at Gawsworth; a spectre in green velvet at Hoghton Tower; six ghosts at East Riddlesden Hall; a headless apparition at Westwood Manor; and then there are some little-known ghosts in Windsor Castle, Hampton Court Palace and the Tower of London, and the strange ghosts of Chingle Hall, perhaps the most haunted house in England.

Exorcism!

Throughout history, the practice of exorcism has been used for the purpose of driving out evil spirits and demons though to possess human beings and the places they inhabit. But there are more startling instances where exorcism has been used: to cure a trawler that seemed to be cursed; to expel demons from Bram Stoker's black 'vampire' dog' even to rid Loch Ness and the Bermuda Triangle of their evil ambience. Peter Underwood explores this frightening ritual in relation to witches, vampires and animals, while his far-flung researches have unearthed dramatic cases in Morocco, Egypt, South Africa and the United States, as well as the British Isles.

Death In Hollywood

The Hollywood way of life has long been a potent

mix of scandal, secrecy and sensation: exactly like the Hollywood way of death...

In this unique study, Peter Underwood charts the lives, loves and deaths of thirty of Tinseltown's most glittering stars. Many deaths were sad or senseless; some were tragic; others were the revenge of old age, while a few were the revenge of something altogether more sinister...

Peter Underwood's Guide To Ghosts & Haunted Places

Based on 50 years' expert study and investigation, this collection of cases from the files of Peter Underwood - an acknowledged expert and experienced investigator of haunted houses - represents a unique exploration of the world of ghosts, apparitions and psychic phenomena. If you want to satisfy your curiosity about the subject or simply enjoy a riveting read, this guide is for you.

No Common Task: The Autobiography Of A Ghost-Hunter

This is the autobiography of a man who has spent thirty-five years of his life covering scientific psychical research, with detailed investigations into all kinds of manifestation that might be supernatural or paranormal in origin, including spiritualism,

ESP, telepathy, hauntings and other occult phenomena. Many of the true experiences from the author's casebook are published here for the first time.

Dictionary Of The Supernatural

An A to Z of Hauntings, Possession, Witchcraft, Demonology and Other Occult Phenomena...

The entries cover all known (and some very little known) organisations, individuals, periodicals, terms of reference, and significant cases, events and incidents relevant to the subject. Under each entry there are notes on other appropriate books and further reading.

The Ghost Hunter's Guide

What are the qualities which make an ideal ghost hunter? You need to be part detective, part investigative reporter, a scientist, with a measure of the psychologist thrown in...

In this book, which is the first real guide to the hunting of ghosts, Peter Underwood manages to cover just about every aspect of this intriguing and mystifying subject.

Jack The Ripper: One Hundred Years Of Mystery

Jack the Ripper still causes a shudder, synonymous as it is with violent murder and mutilation. But also of mystery and speculation - for the gruesome series of killings in London's East End in that horrific Autumn of 1888 have never been finally solved.

The Complete Book Of Dowsing And Divining

This comprehensive volume on dowsing and divining - from the twig and the pendulum to motorscopes and bare hands - traces the story of these fascinating and enigmatic phenomena from its origins in the world of fairy tales and mythology to recent theories that the enigma can be explained in terms of present-day psychology.

Into The Occult

Despite all the answers that conventional science can provide to the earth's mysteries, there remain certain phenomena for which no explanation can yet be found outside the occult. For this reason exploration of the occult and paranormal provides endless fascination.

Here is a survey of all the different aspects of this complex and intriguing subject, including an entire chapter on the relationship between sex and psychic phenomena, a subject on which, until recently, there has been an unwillingness to talk.

Deeper Into The Occult

'In an age when voodoo dancers have appeared in London, when Robert Williams, chief psychologist at Kansas State Industrial Reformatory admits to being a practising war-lock; when moon-astronaut Edgar Mitchell conducts extra sensory experiments in space; when the course of a £1,000,000 road is altered to save a 'fairy tree'; when a ghost is officially registered on a census form; when Americans can 'dial-a-horoscope' for a twenty-four hour prophesy; and when the complete skeleton of a cyclops is unearthed by archaeologists — is it surprising that there is a growing interest in the occult, for research in many fields simply proves that things are not what they seem?'

Nights In Haunted Houses

For over thirty years, in his position as President and Chief Investigator of the Ghost Club of Great Britain, Peter Underwood was actively involved in undertaking night vigils and carrying out research into ghosts and paranormal activity in controlled, scientific conditions.

Queen Victoria's Other World

There have been many books about Queen Victoria but there has never been one that has explored her 'other world' - the world of the strange and unusual, the world of death and her fascination for it, and the world of the unseen and the paranormal that she could never resist.

The Vampire's Bedside Companion: The Amazing World Of Vampires In Fact And Fiction

The Vampire's Bedside Companion is a riveting compendium of new facts and fiction on the 'undying' theme of vampirism.

Here is a new theory on the genesis of Dracula (surely literature's most compelling and macabre figure); thoughts on allusions to vampirism in Wuthering Heights; first-hand experience of Vampires in Hampstead, London; publication for the first time of the story of a fifteenth-century Vampire Protection medallion that Montague Summers presented to the author; an account by a professer of English at Dalhousie University of a visit to 'Castle Dracula' in Transylvania - The Vampire's Bedside Companion contains these and a wealth of other hitherto unpublished material on a subject that is of enduring interest: The Vampire Legend.

The Ghost Hunters: Who They Are And What They Do

A leading psychical researcher takes an in-depth look at ghost hunters, both past and present. Who are these intrepid explorers of the unknown? How do they probe and examine the realms of the seemingly inexplicable? What are their conclusions? In fascinating detail, Peter Underwood profiles the lives and adventures of some of the most famous names in psychical investigation.

The Ghosts Of Borley: Annals Of The Haunted Rectory

'The Ghosts of Borley' (1973) was the first complete record of the unique Borley Rectory hauntings, detailing all the evidence known about this notorious haunted house from the early days of the Rev. H. D. E. Bull who built Borley Rectory in 1863, through the incumbencies of the Rev. Harry Bull, the Rev. Guy Eric Smith and the Rev. Lionel Foyster, to the investigations by Harry Price and other members of the Society for Psychical Research (SPR).

Printed in Great Britain
by Amazon